# HATPINS & HATPIN HOLDERS
## An Illustrated Value Guide

By
Lillian Baker

Color Photography
by
Dave Hammell

**COLLECTOR BOOKS**
P.O. Box 3009
Paducah, KY 42001

The current values in this book should be used only as a guide. They are not intended to set prices, which vary from one section of the country to another. Auction prices as well as dealer prices vary greatly and are affected by condition as well as demand. Neither the Author nor the Publisher assumes responsibility for any losses that might be incurred as a result of consulting this guide.

Additional copies of this book may be ordered from:

COLLECTOR BOOKS
P.O. Box 3009
Paducah, Kentucky 42001

OR

Lillian Baker
15237 Chanera Avenue
Alondra Park, Gardena, California 90249

@$9.95. Add $2.00 for postage and handling.
Copyright: Lillian Baker, 1983
Updated Values 1994

Printed by IMAGE GRAPHICS, INC., Paducah, Kentucky

## COVER CREDITS

Design and layout by Lillian Baker
Photography by Dave Hammell
Collections by Dena Archer, Lillian Baker, & Milly Combs
Silhouette Logo on Back Cover by Wanda G. Baker

## DEDICATION

For
ICC of H&HH
and
R.A.B.

# TABLE OF CONTENTS

# SECTION I.

## CHAPTER I
## INTRODUCTION

## CHAPTER II
## "PERIOD" HATPIN

## CHAPTER III
## SOURCES & MANUFACTURING INFORMATION

## CHAPTER IV
## HOW TO RECOGNIZE & AVOID FAKED HATPINS

## CHAPTER V
## LOOK-ALIKES & REPRODUCTIONS

"Well, you know the old saying -- walk softly and carry a long hatpin . . ."
(THE YEAR OF THE HORSE, Eric Hatch)

## CHAPTER I

### A Brief Introduction to Hatpins:
### Points of Decorative, Functional, and Historical Interest

A hatpin was used to securely fasten a hat to the head of the wearer. Hatpins measuring from 4″ to 12″ in length, were worn from approximately 1850-1930. Because of the size of the hats and the hairstyles, it often required several of these functional pins to defy gravity and whip the whims of capricious winds.

Very little illuminating data about the hatpin has been published. The fascinating history and legal ramifications about this uniquely decorative, functional, and historical piece of jewelry, have been hinted at but rarely detailed. Perhaps because of the hatpin's common usage, it was simply disregarded or overlooked in texts.

This surprising omission can be likened to instructions that appeared in a "do-it-yourself" manual. In this guide, the reader was instructed to "place two pieces of redwood lumber together and hammer". Now because of the common usage of the household nail, it was assumed that the reader knew what to hammer; and thus, when many authors described the sumptuous hats of a bygone era, they erroneously assumed that the reader knew how the hat was secured to the hair and to the head.

The hatpin performed as the most functional and decorative in the pin-family, and certainly exhibited the extraordinary "piece of wire" at its greatest length. So much of the past has been lost because there were few historians who lent enough importance to the simple items in common usage, yet how these self-same investigators rejoice upon discovery of these everyday "tools" in excavations, and how they bemoan the non-existence of manuals.

Here is a handbook to supply the missing manual. The handbook is both a supplemental work to the author's encyclopedia on the subject, as well as a handy handbag or pocket-sized reference book. *The Collector's Encyclopedia of Hatpin and Hatpin Holders*, (COLLECTOR BOOKS, 1976), the only definitive worldwide work on the subject of hatpins and hatpin holders is now out of print, and has itself become a "collectible".

This handbook is somewhat of a digest of the larger work, with further clarification of pertinent facts and new information which has been broadened or simplified to serve both the seasoned and novice collector of hatpins, hatpin holders, and related objects.

The *15th Edition, The Encyclopedia Britannica*, (1975), lists "hatpin" for the first time, and shows it spelled as one word. This is helpful, for it then defines and separates the meaning of "hat pin", (two words), which describes an actual badge worn by men on the hatband of their illustrious headgear from women's jewelry, in the form of hatpins, which is correctly spelled as one word -- HATPIN -- thus making the proper distinction between the male and female uses of this pinning device.

Many people have a preconceived notion that a woman's hatpin resembles a corsage pin, and that these pins may be worn interchangeably. For instance, in *MS* magazine, (Sept. 1972), author Kate Millet, writing about Angela Davis, states: "One almost sees the mark of the hatpin in her lapel where they pinned the corsage." This is a perfect example of the preconceived notion that a corsage pin and a hatpin are one and the same thing. They are not.

The youth of the 20th Century are amused and amazed when viewing an exhibit of collectible period hatpins and hatpin receptacles. In books read by these young people, hatpins are usually referred to as merely "long with fancy knobs at the ends". Or they have, through hearsay or in reading present-day novels, accepted the assigned and unearned description of a hatpin as being a "weapon", instead of a most fanciful and intriguing collectible.

Yet there's a truly fascinating and absorbing history about the hatpin involving much myth and legend, which includes the rise and fall of the feminine hat and headdress. For the historian-purist, here's one of the many interesting points: the assortment of wires used for fastening or ornamentation (or both), includes the common straight pin, pushpin, T-pin, safety pin, brooch, bobby pin, cotter pin, stickpin, veil pin, corsage pin, cape pin, and finally the hatpin. Nothing more has been done with that common wire shaft since the innovation of the period hatpins, circa 1850-1930.

It was the hatpin, of course, that enabled women to discard the bonnet strings and adopt the masculine attire -- a hat -- as their symbol of equality.

When an encyclopedic work appeared a few years back listing the 100 greatest inventions of mankind, it was indeed surprising to find the pin unlisted. Yet the pin has proven to be as near a boon to mankind as the wheel!

The simple cotter pin permitted the successful invention of the automobile, among other advancements; another example of overlooking "things" in common usage. Without pinning devices, there could have been no modern garment industry, and so on and so on.

By 1913, the hatpin had reached the "end of the wire", culminating its functional use at its greatest length and glory. What other piece of jewelry had actual laws written about it? Some of these laws still remain on the books to this day. During the hatpin's brief "period of glory", came some of the most fascinating tales of the hatpin -- a jeweled accessory which surely was the most decorative and functional in the closet of women's fashionable conceits.

This handbook can only touch on the more interesting of the many highlights of a subject so long neglected. Hatpins and their related accessories are not only collectible but are legitimately part of our literature, the theatre, our folklore, and our politics.

The historical, legal, and political ramifications of the hatpin are truly fascinating. Imagine laws which governed the length of hatpins, how they could be worn, and further restrictions placed upon them relative to public accomodations and transportation.

The 1910 headlines and continuing stories reported in the newspapers about hatpins, created the "international hatpin crisis", and the hatpin became society's newest and most dangerous "lethal weapon". This "crisis" would have continued had not an assassin's bullet holed a royal robe, thus precipitating World War I.

As Taylor Caldwell wrote: ". . . Americans were more concerned with the danger of women's hatpins, long and sharp, in streetcars and in crowded places, than with faint murmurs of some horror gathering." (Caldwell was, of course, referring to the gathering of war clouds and the terrible devastation that followed.)

While men fought in wartime trenches, women at the homefront were more fully entrenching the doctrine of "women's rights", a movement begun in time of peace. Today's ERA movement was actually born during the hatpin era, and bred in the Equal Rights Amendment which was defeated in 1982.

In that early struggle for women's suffrage, Miss Harriet Stanton Blatch's letter to the *New York Times*, (1914), read: ". . .in your telegraphic news from Paris recently we are informed that edicts have been issued twice against unprotected hatpins, but that the *Parisienne* merely smiles and goes her way." Miss Blatch referred to the Chief of Paris police as one who was "held in terror by the Apache", but who could not hold the fort in his own gay Paris where pointed "arrows" darted out from women's fashionable hats.

"This is", her letter continued, "but another argument for Votes for Women and another painful illustration of the fact that men cannot discipline women . . . Give women political power and the best among them will gradually train the uncivilized, just as the best among men have trained their sex . . ."

Woman's Suffrage and the ERA are good and current points of reference, for the hatpin was involved in the movement created by our very first "feminists". It is an historical fact that the hat is the true symbol of woman's emancipation. That is, the wearing of a hat. This political symbol was made possible by the advent of the pin-making machine in 1832. This man-made invention was the mechanical device that forever changed the course of man, material, and women.

This ingenious machine not only permitted all sorts of pinning devices for machines, but one of its greatest virtues was that pointed "tool" with which women were able to adopt the hat, their liberation from bonnetstrings and apronstrings.

The pin has always been taken much too much for granted. Prior to the 1832 invention of that pin-making device little over a century and a half ago, the stealing of handmade pins was a hanging offense. Taxes were levied to pay for the Queen's pins, and the purchase of handmade pins by her subjects was limited to the first day of the New Year. So, women saved for that "pin-day", the origin of the expression, "pin money". In fact, pins were so expensive and treasured, the handmade variety were named in bequests and legacies.

Until the pin-making machine, pins were handmade, and it took seven men to make a single pin. Elizabeth Barrett Browning put it poetically, and with moral objectivity, in her writings, to wit:

". . . Let us be content, in work,
To do the thing we can, and not presume
To fret because it's little. 'Twill employ
Seven men, they say, to make a perfect pin:
Who makes the head, content to miss the point;
Who makes the point, agreed to leave the join;
And if a man should cry, 'I want a pin,
And I must make it straightway, head and point,'
His wisdom is not worth the pin he wants.
Seven men to a pin -- and not a man too much!"

The hat has been referred to several times hence, as a "symbol" of woman's emancipation. The hat, from the beginning of time, was more than a mere head-covering. It was the symbol of ones station in life -- or more correctly -- man's station. We are all familiar with the expression, "He wore many hats". Until the manufactured hatpin, *he* was a literal designation, for women had no "station" other than that realm of subservience from which the early suffragettes sought emancipation.

Indeed, no woman wore a hat; she was confined beneath a hood, wimple, hennin, or a bonnet with strings drawn tightly under her chin. And it was in the loosening and the eventual cutting of those bonnet strings that women cut away from the hearth and the home and the "queendom" they ruled often in nameless obscurity.

In the wider challenge of the so-called "man's world", men were recognized and duly respected by the various hats they wore. The king has his crown. The baker, the tailor, the miner, even the shepherd had his recognizable hat or head covering. The biblical Shadrach, Meshach, and Abednego kept their dignity by walking into the blazing furnace with their hats on.

Now there are early paintings that portray women wearing plumed hats, large and small, but these were styled like those worn by the noblemen of their day. These daring women were the darlings of the court -- the "jet set" of their day -- and when they lost favor, it was off with both head and hat!

With the Machine Age and the Industrial Revolution of the 19th century, women came out of the Victorian parlor into the parlor-cars which rattled on new-laid railroad tracks across the continent.

The shocking use of public transportation by "emancipated women" caused many new problems, including "the hatpin danger". In America and in Europe, laws required that "all dangerous points of hatpins be covered by guards".

The Paris Mail, (1909), reported: ". . . From Illinois: To limit the length of women's hatpins to nine inches, and make them take out permits for longer ones, just like all deadly weapons".

Interestingly enough, closed-vestibule railroad passenger cars had not been in general use until 1900, and the "street railway" in America had begun in 1888. The New York "elevated" rumbled overhead in 1883, and the wider use by women of these modes of transportation, introduced perfect strangers -- male and female -- who were reported to be "touching and brushing" each other. The protruding hatpin in such close quarters did, indeed, become a physical danger and a heated point of controversy.

But women refused to give up the wearing of hats, and the adopted hats -- the more ostentatious the better -- required the use of several long, pointed, hatpins. Women also adopted a hairstyle which allowed her tresses to be shown in full abundancy. Until woman's entry into the business and political world, only virtuous maidens wore their hair unbound, adorned with flowers and coronets, the better to entice the opposite gender. Once married, woman's hair was drawn, quartered, and knotted under mobcaps and bonnets, for it became her husband's province alone to see her "crowning glory" loosened in the privacy of the boudoir.

A little more than a half-century ago, London's popular *The Daily Mail*, (1908), printed a story about the jailed suffragettes, those venturesome women who were ordered to appear before the Bench with rather unusual restrictions. It seems there was some fear in the courtroom of "a dangerous attack of pin-pricks", and thus came the order that ". . . women prisoners of Clerkenwell Sessions were allowed to appear in hats but without hatpins".

We have only to study the fashion plates of that day to realize this order to remove hatpins necessitated the removal of hats. And a removal of hats was tantamount to a forfeiture of dignity, for no lady would be seen bare-headed in public, no less a courtroom. Of course the suffragettes could not remove their hatpins without causing their hats to fall askew. To require them to remove their hatpins and subsequently their hats, was as gross as insisting that His Honor, the Magistrate, remove the wig which lent dignity to his position on the Bench.

If the suffragettes had intended using their hatpins as "weapons", they would have done so when resisting arrest, or against their jailors. But, in fact, these noble women were mainly of middle or upper-crust polite society. Only women of the slums used their hatpins in neighborhood squabbles.

Was there a precedent for this Magistrate's order? Surely no judge, by mere whim, could order the removal of any portion of ones clothing without some "legal" precedent. Perhaps the edict regarding the ordered removal of hatpins in the courtroom at Clerkenwell Sessions, came about because of the past performance of the Athenian women who were deprived of their stiletto pins owing to the deadly use they made of them.

Legend tells us that following the catastrophe at ancient Thermopylae, (480 B.C.), where 300 brave Spartans fought for three successive days against the Persians, only one Spartan returned alive to Athens. The wives of those soldiers who had fallen in battle were so angered that a sole warrior had escaped when their own spouses had been killed, they attacked the survivor *en masse*. They stabbed him to death with the bodkins with which the ladies' tunics were fastened. This unprecedented behavior led to a different mode of dress being imposed upon them which did not require large pins; instead the tunics were tied or laced at the shoulder.

Poet James Jeffrey Roche makes a reference to that episode in *The Men of the Alamo*, (Poems of American History):

"Thermopylae left one alive --
The Alamo left none."

Was the magistrate at Clerkenwell Sessions remembering the vengence of the Athenian women? Or, under the guise of "pin pricks", was he attempting to create a comic, chaotic media event out of women's attempt to gain the vote?

Whatever the judge's motive, his action merely propelled the suffragette movement, especially in America where women had already adopted hats of outlandish proportion. Women's chapeau increased in size until some hats actually shadowed the shoulders of the wearer, and theatre doors had to be widened to accomodate entry.

By World War I, less than a quarter of a century after the incident at Clerkenwell Sessions, the Machine Age set the die, and no longer was man or woman an "island unto himself". No more were the social, political, economic, or private worlds of the individual or family as it once was: male-dominated and male-orientated.

And to think it was the collectible hatpin that contributed to this remarkable change and chain of events that have since followed its usage.

## CHAPTER II
## What Is A "Period" Hatpin?

*"Don't forget to speak scornfully of the Victorian Age, there will*
*be time enough for meekness when you try to better it."*
(Sir James Matthew Barrie, author "Peter Pan", [1860-1937])

As necessity is the mother of invention and ingenuity, so was born the hatpin of the Victorian Age, a decorative instrument never quite equalled in individuality of style or function.

Pins, in general, have withstood the tests of time and progress, but the exception must truly be the period hatpin. This pin, with its exceptional length, was utilized for such a short span of years and yet was an ingenious combination of utility and ornament.

The height of the hatpin era was the period from 1890 through 1925, and therefore it's more than coincidence that the influence in design should be that of the Aesthetic Period, the Arts and Crafts Movement, Art Nouveau, and the Art Deco eras. The dating of the latter two, meshes just prior to World War I.

Even before these decorative periods, came the earlier Victorian influence which embraced the innovations of gothic elaborations, including elegant formal scrolls, ingenious openwork and filigree with baroque renderings highly influenced -- indeed, almost copied -- from ancient Etruscan and Greek realms of jewelry-making.

Hatpins manufactured from 1850-1925, are the collectible "period" hatpins. Without inviting repetition, we know that from 1861, Queen Victoria popularized jet during her extended period of mourning, and that the genuine jet -- the finest coming from the Whitby area near Yorkshire, England -- was quickly imitated in both French and Bohemian glass. The jet imitations, like other renditions in fine paste, were no less extraordinary in craftsmanship and design than were the genuine pieces. Only microscopic examination by an expert jeweler-gemologist can separate the real from the substitute article, for these man-made materials were in truth substitutes produced to satisfy mass production at prices "the masses" could afford to pay.

The Victorian jeweler was an expert craftsman and his works challenge those that came before and after his time. Because of this recognized distinction, a large quantity of Victorian hatpins are delightful, intriguing renditions of the jeweler's art.

The substitutes for jet, gemstones, and gems, were never intended as a "lesser" batch of jewels, but as a tribute to man's ingenuity in imitating and reproducing natural elements and materials. The workmanship in glass jet or French paste, was equivalent to that demonstrated in finely faceted diamonds, rubies, and emeralds. Certainly the variations in cut and/or molded glass after it had been applied to the tin-wheel, are even more diverse for there was no expensive risk as when working with the genuine gems and gemstones. [The term "gems" and "gemstones", is used rather than "precious" and "non-precious" stones for two reasons: 1) tastes change, and a once popular stone may have fallen from favor or vice-versa, thus increasing or decreasing its monetary value; 2) it is accepted in the trade that diamonds, rubies, sapphires, and emeralds are classified as "precious gems"; traditionally, all others had been considered "semi-precious". The times now seem to dictate that all gems and gemstones are "precious", according to ones individual taste or preference. The art of glassmaking is being more fully appreciated as well, and faceted glass stones are receiving due recognition at long last.]

We know that prior to 1832, small handmade pins with decorative heads were used as devices to secure lace caps, mob-caps, veils and other pinnings to head and body attire. We also realize that it was not until the introduction of stringless "bonnets" that the PERIOD HATPIN entered the scene. Both the transition from bonnet to hat, and the introduction of plentiful hatpins were due, in part, to the less expensive machine-made hatpins which were manufactured "by the ton".

The hatpin heads, in 1850, and the length of the pinshanks, were both small and short with their gothic-type ornaments of either silver, gold, or patterned glass. The metals were encrusted with gems and gemstones with a beginning emphasis on "non-precious" gems such as topaz, amethyst, coral, and such. Of course there later came the introduction of even more unfamiliar gems utilized by the great innovators of the Art Nouveau period.

Nothing influenced change in fashions -- including headgear -- as did the social and political upheavals which seemed to arrive with the Machine Age. Die-stamping superceded hand-wrought custom-made pieces of jewelry, and new scientific discoveries, (including the all-important harnessing of electricity), created an evolution in manufacturing and a revolution of peoples against traditional values -- moral and material.

Sometime into the fourth decade of the 19th century, the English firm of Elkington patented an electroplating process for coating base metal with silver or gold. Pinchbeck became *passe'*, and the "nobility of gems" was enjoyed by "the masses" for the first time. Let the nobel jewel be "plated" or of imitation paste, for jewelry was made to be worn, not weighed for worth.

Meanwhile the exhibitions of unique jewelers' works were a great influence world-wide, with each country not above copying "the masters". Thus, it's difficult even today to attribute unmarked pieces to a particular country or "cult". So varied were these copies, that only a very few "eccentric" designers and jewelers survived in their own right, and have been acclaimed both within and outside their homelands.

Up until the Art Deco period, (1910-1925), early craftsmanship shows the use of heavier electro-deposit on Victorian and Edwardian jewelry, including hatpin and hair ornaments. This is most apparent to anyone handling a collection of period hatpins of that 1850-1910 era. These pieces were made to last, unlike much of the tin-like substances offered in today's mass-produced jewelry.

As hats became wider and bolder, and hair was shown in more abundant quantities, the necessary securing implement, the hatpin, became longer and surely as opulent as the millinery itself.

Much of the Victorian vintage jewelry was manufactured in Derby and Birmingham, England, although it would be difficult to detect whether such articles originated in Frankfurt or Hanau, Germany, Paris, or Valenza Po, or in Rome. Because of the "internationalism" which had been a feature of jewelry ever since the publication of jewelry pattern books in the 16th century, most hatpins cannot be ascribed to any exact date or even to the country of origin. An exception, perhaps, is the glass molded hatpins which came from button manufacturers, for many of these can be traced to American catalogues, as well as those of Germany, France, and Bohemia.

But as for hatpins of metallic composition, only those which are hallmarked or trademarked, can truly be authenticated for date and origin. Hatpins which were custom-made and created by master-jewelers, are better identified because of the distinctive lines, enamelling, or other unique application which distinguish the rare artist and his craft.

No pin in the celebrated pin-family is more deserving of the definition: ". . . a stop to limit the motion of some moving piece . . .", than does the period hatpin. What else prevented the complete toppling-over of those millinery masterpieces? Just as an easel holds the canvas upright and steady, so hatpins secured and fastened the hat to the head. But it is misleading for some to report that the hatpin was invented to "hold the hat onto the high-piled pompadour hair styles", for the "pompadour" preceded the Victorian and Gibson-Girl hairplay.

The true pompadour hair style of its era was decorated with jewels, flowers, fan-fare and elaborate hair decorations including fancy lace caps. Caps were, indeed, the forerunners of women's hats, but the first hat -- which was of felt, wasn't introduced in America until 1851. No doubt there were earlier examples of "hats" on the Continent since fashion dictates arrived from European shores to American shores. Prior to the stylish introduction of hats, women were "confined" to wearing bonnets securely tied under the chin. When the bonnetstrings were unfastened, the strings were left flapping in the breeze, and were called "lappets". To help keep the bonnet straight on the head, small "bonnet pins" were sold for the first time, and the pin-heads were modest in design.

The famed Providence, R.I., firm, Gorham Manufacturing Co., made many Victorian baroque-style sterling silver hatpins from the late sixties through 1887, and these suited the modest tastes of early-Victoriana. Gorham's hatpins were distributed by Spaulding & Co., (Chicago); Black, Starr & Frost, (New York); and Shreve & Co., (San Francisco).

When the popularity of Art Nouveau became apparent to the trade, Gorham joined other jewelry manufacturers in the production of hatpins of the latter 19th century, catering to the whims and pocketbook of "the masses".

Eventually, the hatpin was made of every natural and manufactured element in a myriad of designs, enough to challenge the most vivid imagination. They were contrived to serve every fashion need and complemented the milliner's art.

Collectors of period hatpins can zero in on one specific type, i.e., handpainted porcelains, sterling silver, commemoratives, sporting activities, Carnival Glass, Art Nouveau and/or Art Deco designs, Victorian gothics accented with finely faceted glass stones, exquisite rhinestone hatpins, estcucheon engraved and brass-mounted heads, gold and gems, or simply primitive types made in the Victorian parlor or for the millinery trade.

Some collectors prefer the long pins, while others select one-of-a-kind gold or silver embedded with gems. Others seek out tremblants or nodder-type hatpins.

A NOMENCLATURE FOR PERIOD HATPINS can be found in that section of the handbook.

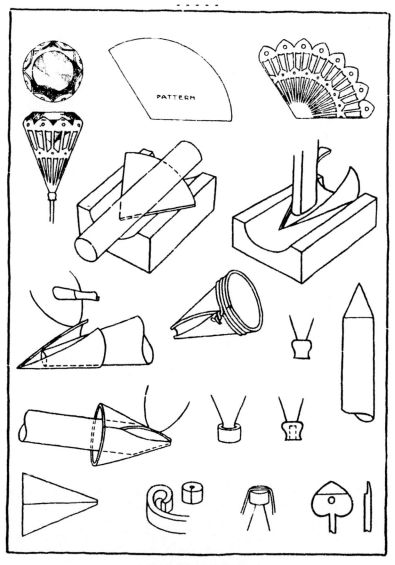

**MAKING A HATPIN**
*Jewelry Making and Design*, Plate XXIII, A. Rose and A. Cirino, Metal Crafts Publ., Providence, R.I. (1917). [Courtesy B.K. Zwartjes-van Spanje, The Netherlands]

# CHAPTER III
## THE PERIOD HATPIN:
## SOME SOURCES & MANUFACTURING INFORMATION

Authorities on costume and headdress often differ as to the dating of the first hatpins. Bill Severn wrote: ". . . Long hatpins, especially made for the purpose of holding in place large summer straw hats with drooping brims, first came into use in the 1850's. They were soon followed by jeweled-topped hatpins to replace the long ties of ribbon that had been used to hold women's hats on their heads . . . the pins often stuck out several inches beyond the hat brim".

The "large summer straw hats with drooping brims", may well have been designed after the Gainsborough hat -- named for the 18th century painter -- but the great difference was that the 19th century "summer hat" was set atop a new hairstyle which required cotton batting, wires, and false hair to make them into "towering tresses". Atop this mass sat the chapeau, pinned on with the necessary "equipment" of 19th century manufactured anchorage which secured all to the head. Many of the horsehair cushions or "rats" were quite heavy, as were the cotton or wool "foundations" upon which the hair was built up to be stylish.

Many hatpins were required to keep these extra additions pinned to the head. Before the manufactured pins, hand-made hair pins were also expensive, and therefore "ladies kept their hair in place with a sort of gum or mucilage; the bourgeoise used a paste made of dust of rotten oak, and the peasant used flour".

Although bent wire hair pins were known as early as the 16th century, they were all hand wrought, as were the hatpins before the advent of the pin-making machine in 1832. As if fated to be joined, the manufacture of artificial flowers was perfected at the same time and commercialized in France, especially by the dressmakers and the milliners who saw a good thing when they "sewed" it. Thus, as hats came into their own, they were bedecked with a wide range of flowers and brash ornaments. "Commercial enterprise" produced an electrifying progression of movements for the "betterment of women", and most of these emerged from the Fashion Front.

Because the pin-machine had not yet been invented during the ill-fated reign of Louis XVI's Queen of France, Marie Antoinette, her famed caps and bonnets trimmed with yards and yards of pearls and veilings were kept in place with the delicate hand-made, short, wire hair pins and the double-pronged veil pins of that period. These were worn in such great numbers that it is reported the closely pinned hair ornaments looked and sparkled like the heavens on a crisp, clear, Christmas Eve.

Hatpins of any size, and with the MANUFACTURED pin, did not invade the fashion scene until after 1832. The pins prior to that time -- pins used for pinning wimples, hennins, lace-caps, and other headcoverings for women -- resembled today's common straight pin rather than a hatpin.

The period hatpin surely challenged man's ingenuity, for women demanded an ever-increasing variety in shapes, sizes, and settings. Name the media, and it has been used in the making and manufacture of hatpins.

Who met this challenge? How was it met? Let's touch upon this wide field of endeavor.

In America there was Louis C. Tiffany of New York, William J. Codman of Providence, and the American "clique" comprising James T. Wooley (formerly of England), Barton P. Jenks, and George C. Gebelein. These were some of the craftsmen who made and/or designed metallic hatpins. They yielded the field of glass-headed hatpins to the famous New Jersey, Ohio, and Massachusettes factories producing Victorian glassware and buttons.

In 1878, Louis Comfort Tiffany, son of the well-known jeweler, established C. Tiffany Company which then expanded in 1892, to Tiffany Glass and Decorating Company. His firm catered to wealthy clientele whose tastes were along Victorian baroque elegance. There were, no doubt, those women among his customers who were intrigued with deviations in the jewelry line, but they were few enough so that Tiffany was not too well represented in the up-and-coming Art Nouveau hatpin movement -- except in his unique glass. It is here that Louis Comfort Tiffany excelled and left his permanent mark in the decorative field.

From 1900 to 1936, Tiffany Studios of New York, which was merely a continuation of the older firm of Tiffany and Co., did produce lovely hatpins which often lacked the traditional markings found on Tiffany's lovely glassware. Some hatpins were sold in plush boxes which were imprinted but did not have an identifying mark on the hatpin(s). Other hatpins were simply marked "Tiffany", without jeweler's hallmarks; but many of these can be recognized as the work typical of the company and artist.

An exhibition at Boston, Mass., 1897, brought about a swift

change and rapid public demand for Art Nouveau designed hatpins and most of these were made in silver.

The American silver companies which were major manufacturers of such hatpins for the masses, were: Unger Bros., (Newark, N.J.); The Sterling Company and Alvin Manufacturing Co., (Providence, R.I.); and the R. Blackinton & Co., (North Attleboro, Mass.), another major jewelry center in America.

Other American companies included: J.E. Caldwell & Co., (Philadelphia, Pa.); F.M. Whiting & Co., (N. Attleboro, Mass.); William B. Kerr & Co., (Newark, N.J.); R. Wallace & Sons, (Providence, R.I.); Reed & Barton, (Providence, R.I.); Hyatt Brothers, (Newark, N.J.), who were exponents of the wonderful Art Deco celluloid hatpins; and Woodside Sterling, and Mauser Manufacturing companies of America's major jewelry metropolis, New York.

From F.H. Noble & Co., Chicago, founded in 1876, came the necessary jewelers' findings which were utilized by the manufacturers of the ornamental hatpin heads. Individual jewelry craftsmen were much concerned with the artistic merit of the hatpin ornament, and not with the utilitarian parts which secured the ornaments to the varied lengths of pin-wire. The findings were therefore manufactured as a component part, and not by the jeweler himself. Many pin manufacturing firms in Providence and Attleboro were the suppliers of these essential pieces, and still make various "findings" today. Their names and lineage in the "yellow pages", reads like an historical document.

Most hatpins by the above manufacturers were of the popular Art Nouveau and Art Deco styles of the 1890-1925 era. Many of the hatpins were ordered through jewelers' catalogues or through the popular Montgomery, Ward & Co., and the Sears, Roebuck and Co.; but the hatpins in the latter catalogues did not feature domestic merchandise but rather advertised "imported Parisian" merchandise -- no doubt for "snob-appeal" which was as prevalent then as it seems to exist today.

The major American centers for custom and costume jewelry were New York, Providence, Philadelphia, and both Attleboro and North Attleboro. Archives and company records reveal very little historical information regarding design and manufacture of hatpins. However, we can piece together some half-lucid image of the hatpin era with these conjectures:

29

The flamboyant hatpin period certainly arrived by 1890, and by 1905, the Art Nouveau influence in design was felt in decoratives which included hair ornaments and the hatpin.

Art Nouveau reached its height by 1910, being pushed from the scene with the advent of worldwide social and political upheaval. But this "brief encounter" met with such giants as America's Louis Comfort Tiffany, Austria's Gustave Limpt, Belgium's Velde and Horta, England's C.R. Ashbee and other jeweler-designers working anonymously for Liberty & Co., and Charles Horner, Ltd.; and then there were men of genius such as R. Lalique, who left an impression which is gaining a renewed appreciation and revival today by both professional and layman alike.

It was the Art Nouveau period which produced the finest examples of hatpins, those that are considered highly collectible. Millinery "madness" of that era required multiples of hatpins, many with the longest pin-stems for the sumptuous hats not since matched for millinery perfection and creativity.

Who were these intrepid artists and designers who gave hatpin collectors their prized tableau of Art Nouveau hatpins? They were not the artists who began their craft in this famed period, but had joined with its founders and innovators: Charles Robert Ashbee of Britain and his countryman, William Morris (of Arts and Crafts Movement fame). The birthplace of Art Nouveau was in their Arts and Crafts center, the 1888 School of Handicraft, which in turn bore the romantic influence of Walter Crane (1880), John Ruskin, his contemporary, and the mark of that unpredictable virtuoso of pen-and-ink, Aubrey Beardsley.

*The Studio* magazine, London's monthly publication from 1893 into the 20th century, was greatly responsible for the public acceptance of the startling Art Nouveau designs and the influence of the artistic work pictured therein was felt on both sides of the Atlantic.

All the arts are brothers under the media, so to speak, and the natural influence of "blood-relation" cannot be denied in the Art Nouveau movement. What was rendered on one-dimensional paper could be seen in all-dimensional jeweler's fabric of metal and stone.

The Paris Exposition, 1900, which featured the fantastic work of Art Nouveau artists from America and the Continent, were copied willy-nilly by the large jewelry houses whose mass-produced items, 1890-1920, had the expert finishing touch of individual craftsmen, unlike the mass-produced pieces we know today. In yesteryear, the human hand and eye were the "quality control" factors, and perfection was demanded by both the worker and the boss.

Although America quickly adopted the term "Art Nouveau" from the Parisian establishment of Siegfried Bing's "L'Art Nouveau", (1895), other countries called the "new art":

In Austria: "Weiner Secession", for Weiner Werkstatten, (Arts & Crafts, 1903), founded by Koloman Moser and Josef Hoffman. In other sections of Bohemia, (Czech.), it was known as "Recession Period", or "Secession".

In Germany: "Jugendstil", after the art magazine, "Jugend", (Youth).

In Belgium: Henri Van de Velde and Victor Horta simply worked under the influence of "the movement".

In Italy: "Stile Liberty", named for London's Liberty & Co., department store.

It all began in Britain, despite the French moniker, with Matthew Boulton's Victorian pieces being challenged by the field of Art Nouveau proponents and their followers. Glasgow had Charles Renni MacKintosh, and the Scottish and British clan were copied across the channel by Josef Hoffman of Austria, who was certainly influenced by the designs of Gustave Klimpt. Theodore van Gosen and J.M. Olbrich, joined Hoffman in the trend, while Luca von Cranach and Carl Gross in the German manufacturing town of Pforzheim (with over 1,000 jewelry firms), set the standard there. Holland had Jan Toorop; Italy, V. Miranda, who was eagerly copied by manufacturers in the major jewelry center of Valenza Po.

A bit to the north in Spain, was Julio Gonzales, (1910-1923), who trailed the Art Nouveau movement, yet reflected its effect in his designs; and to the colder north was Georg Jensen of Denmark, who influenced his compatriots, Johan Rohde and Eric Magnussen, right on up into the wonderful Art Deco Period.

Seemingly, only Russia remained on the see-saw between the *risque* development of Art Nouveau and the demand of Russian nobility for the classically ornate rococo and baroque in jewels. This is readily seen in Russia's most famous jewelry house, Carl Peter Faberge and his dynasty of dimensional jewels. But we, as hatpin collectors, are interested in his lovely enamel "little things" such as hatpins, which although unmarked, are easily recognized and attributed to the master enamelling and creativity of the Faberge jewelers.

In the author's recent publication, *Art Nouveau & Art Deco Jewelry*, (Collector Books, Paducah, KY, 1981), there are lists of jewelers, jewelry designers, makers, manufacturers, and retailers in the Chapter headed: THUMBNAIL SKETCHES. There is no doubt that many of those listed contributed to the production of hatpins.

One of the more notable is CHARLES HORNER, the Halifax-based manufacturer using the Chester Hallmark. This is the English firm that pioneered Art Nouveau jewelry on a grand scale specifically for mass distribution. Prized pieces especially coveted by hatpin collectors, are hatpins of sterling designed in the Celtic line, with thistle-cut and faceted stones, and exquisite peacock enamels.

LIBERTY & CO., (1875-     ), founded by Arthur Lasenby Liberty, was a major force in promoting the "new art" in Britain, America, and the Continent. W.H. Haseler Co., located in Birmingham, mass-produced hatpins for LIBERTY & CO., in silver "Cymric" design. The Celtic designs, originated by a score of well-known designers, were sold under the LIBERTY & CO. trademark. Working anonymously were artist-jeweler-designers: Archibald Knox, Arthur Gaskin, Fred Partridge, William Hutton, Edgar Simpson, Oliver Baker, Gertrude Smith, Kate Harris, Jesse M. King, J. Paul Cooper, and Henry Wilson.

Jesse Marion King, (1866-1949), was greatly influenced by the Scottish "Glasgow School of Art", and specialized in designing "Cymric" jewelry for LIBERTY & CO.; "Cymric" was the trade name used by this company for its mass-produced designs from the English Arts and Crafts movement. The jewelry, including hatpins, was then mass-marketed with great success.

Rene Lalique, (1860-1945), was the French innovator of "high" Art Nouveau jewelry, and one of his magnificent hatpins is in the collection of the Kunstindustrimuseet, Copenhagen, Denmark. Unfortunately, few examples of his hatpins exist, as many were converted into other types of jewelry, such as brooches and pendants.

Lalique was apprenticed to Louis Aucoc in 1876, and also worked for Cartier and Boucheron jewelry firms where he was an independent jeweler to the trade. In 1895, Lalique produced his first nude female figure in jewelry; at the 1900 Exposition Universelle Internationale, his entire jewelry production was purchased and is now exhibited at Gulbenkian Foundation, Libson. There are no examples of hatpins at Lisbon, although Lalique designed exquisite hairpins and combs of extraordinary inventiveness.

By 1911, Lalique phased out his jewelry-making after receiving a contract to supply glass containers for the Paris-based firm of Coty perfumers. Lalique glass objects are much sought after, and although one of the most collectible hatpins would be a signed Lalique, the Art Nouveau jeweled pins of George and Jean Fouquet are much treasured. The latter beautifully executed in precious ore, the designs of Alphonse Mucha.

The little-heralded Maurice Dufrene, (1876-1955), who came up at the close of the period and on into the Art Deco years, made superb renderings which lent themselves as prototypes for other jewelry manufacturers. The graphic designs of M.P. Verneuil and Georges Auriol were utilized by jewelers, as were the designs of lesser known artists of the period.

The exciting and influential exhibitions held in Paris, (1900), and in the boutique Compagnie des Arts Fracais, (1919), (owned by Louis Sue and Andrae Mare) turned the knob and pushed open the door to the Art Deco period.

Egyptian motifs have always been popular jewelry designs, but the rage in fashion created by the discovery of The Valley of the Kings and the opening of King Tutankhamen's tomb (1920), was clearly to emphasize and renew the Egyptian influence in design.

Geschutzt is a trademark found in a jet-glass mold of an Egyptian scarab, one of many versions of the beetle depicted in various colored glass hatpins.

Thus the vogue of the twenties brought in the deluge of Art Deco which was mathematical in design based on the triangle, hexagon, and other fascinating equations. Art Deco can easily be separated and identified from the "high" Art Nouveau which was the first breakaway from Victorian "stays" of fashion and design.

The Sphinx, Pharoh, and Cleopatra's royal Asp, were part and parcel of the Art Deco scheme in designing fashions and accessories, including the hatpin. It is easy to see the contrast in

Art Deco stylized, geometric patterns, when compared with the Art Nouveau ornamentation of Alphonse Marie Mucha (1860-1939), Maurice Pillard Verneuil, (1869-1934), Georges Auriol (1863-1938), and Rene Lalique (1860-1945). These artists, whether working in glass or jewelry, incorporated the sinuous lines of the female figure and nature's curlicues which are found in florals. They grasped in graphics the imaginative, flighty, fanciful, ornate butterflies, birds, and creatures of a fantasy-world. And these ideals were produced as hatpin ornaments or decorative and functional accessories. For Art Nouveau is fantasy epitomized; Art Deco is geometrically comprised of an abstract design seemingly bizarre in motif.

This Art Deco abstract diversion invaded the realm of Art Nouveau about 1910, and finally conquered all interest with the opening of those Egyptian tombs, the beginning of trade-in-earnest with Asian, Indian, and Arabic countries, and the overwhelming industrial revolution with its symbolic "speed" and quickening of pace.

It was Japanese art which was beginning to come to the Continent through the recently open-door-trade between East and West that generated the first spark of interest which created the Art Nouveau movement. But Art Nouveau was short-lived, (1895-1910); yet it profoundly stirred the imagination of artists in every field of endeavor. The Art Deco period, (1910-1925), was in reality an extension of Art Nouveau, except that because of previously mentioned factors, the designs changed from the senuous curvilear lines to a compromise between straight, stilted renditions and intervals of trills or frills of its parent-motif.

Not until Art Deco reached maturity, (1920), did it completely break away from Art Nouveau design, and by 1925 Art Deco was already newly named, "Art Moderne". The latter nomenclature extended not only to jewelry and hatpins, which are part of the trade, but to all things industrial. As for the hatpin, what with bobbed hair and the cloche' hat the fashion, the hatpin became nothing more than an ornament which the Art Deco-ists and Modern-ists managed to vault into the annals of absurdities. But then 1925-1940 was an absurd age. It was much like an incubus emerging without knowing whether to crawl, walk, or fly. So it did all three! Examine some of the hat ornaments of the 1926-1940 era, and you will surely have to agree.

In all fairness, Art Deco did not completely abandon the florals, fungals, insects, seaweed, billowing smoke, and other sensual motifs of the Art Nouveau period; rather Art Deco tamed the endless "wanderings" of curvilear lines into strict obedience to the stylized "speed" motifs based on geometric renditions caged in borders of surreal motifs.

The conflict between machine and nature is evident everywhere in Art Deco youth and Art Moderne maturity. There were no such confines in Art Nouveau, which is perhaps why the "new art" was so short-lived. It seems that anything without discipline runs wild and destroys itself by its own exhaustive free-for-all-design. But this child-like freedom, which by its very term is short-lived, is still so terribly touching in the rendition of Art Nouveau women with flowing locks; florals that are moved by an invisible force; insects that discard their biological garb and embrace the once-scorned "inferior" gemstones or paste and combine with man-made enamels that challenge nature's textures and colors.

The flames of Art Nouveau were destined to burn themselves out in the roar and intensity of a newly ignited inspiration. And all this is preserved for us and for future generations in some of the finest examples of hatpins and hat ornaments.

Of course some of the most beautiful and sought-after hatpins are also copied in design from antique jewelry, especially those of Roman and Greek gems. Many of the settings for gems and gemstones are baroque or tend toward the rococo of the 17th and 18th centuries, consisting of an imitation of shells, scrolls, leaves, and exaggerated floral design. Others are neo-classic; several far advanced and more acceptable as abstract in today's evaluation of art. Others, with baton-cut stones cut in the shape of a long, narrow rectangle girdled at its lower edge by a mounting, could challenge the designs of Aubrey Beardsley and his graphic Art Nouveau style. All these renderings appear in collectible hatpins.

Hatpins were often duplicated from original designs executed in genuine gems, by using elaborate heads of paste or colored glass so brilliant they could be mistaken for the precious stones. The colorless paste, not used until the late 19th century, was truly a substitute rather than an imitation of precious gems. These hatpins, made of non-precious materials, were much in demand to suit the prevailing fashions. Some paste which contained a high percentage of lead, could easily be taken for the natural diamond, especially when it had been faceted with the extreme care of the expert craftsman-jeweler.

This paste, or *strass*, was invented in the 18th century by a German goldsmith-jeweler, Josef Strasser. But it was the French paste that surpassed that of others and the periods of Louis XV and XVI have been noted as "the golden age of paste", for it was worn by the aristocracy as a substitute for true gems.

Some of the glass stones set into hatpin heads, are backed with a bright polished foil, a thin leaf of metal placed in back of a gemstone or glass to heighten the brilliance or the color. It's difficult, unless one is an expert, to always distinguish between diamonds, spinels, or a good paste stone.

Period hatpins are also collected by those who fancy the crochet ornaments, beaded heads, braided or polished straw, woven raffia, woven hair of a loved one, and fine needlepoint work. These are known as "primitives".

Hatpin gift sets, which were very popular courting items, included paired hatpins, collar buttons and blouse studs, belt buckles of matching design, as well as veil pins or violet pins with which a corsage could be pinned to a cape, shoulder-strap, or ulster.

The sea provided the abalone pearl in its familiar blister shape and startling iridescence, and the opalescent inner shell of pearl mollusk commonly called "Mother of Pearl". These were combined with seed pearls or crystal, or were set to advantage in a variety of mountings. Eventually, man-made "pearls" from the Bohemian area were shipped by the ton to fashionable Paris and London and were utilized in the hair and for dress decorations, as well as ornamental heads for hatpins. The imitation pearls had a wax-bead base.

Many hatpin settings can be readily detected as designs borrowed from all art styles of the past decades. Romanesque, Gothic, and Renaissance were most favored and the main sources for all hatpin art of the Victorian, Edwardian, and Art Nouveau periods. Right smack in the middle of the Art Nouveau period, came 1897, when the conflagration against the configurations of hat contours arose. Shall the hat be worn high or low?

This was a serious issue for the fashion-conscious society not yet embroiled in political and social unrest. A compromise was reached which resulted in the wearing of both -- the high crowned hats being called "three storeys", and the flat-crowned named "basement hat". Either design was worn upon puffed-up tresses and required the use of several long hatpins.

The hairstyles then required so much artificial hair and "frizzettes", (custom-made toupees), that one company alone was reported to have filled orders at the rate of two tons of "hair merchandise" in a week. Upon this bounty of real and artificial hair, rode a millinery "mast" anchored by several stout hatpins. Chapeaux were complemented with fur, fringe, braid and beads sewn in endless combinations along with silk, chenille, moire, damask, gros grain, metallic thread, and taffeta -- all stitched on felt or straw or heavy velvet -- with the final fashion necessity of hatpins, hatpins, hatpins!

Other unusual hatpins which are *eurekas* to collectors, are ivory-carved, and the 19th century art form of Satsuma with its mellow ivory-tinted porcelain. The fine enamel colors of Indian red, green, blue, purple, black and yellow, with gilding and silvering, are excellent examples of the minutely painted hatpin known as Satsuma-ware. These hatpins are exquisite miniature paintings and are rather scarce and difficult to find. Many Satsuma buttons, knobs, Shoji-screen or rice-paper weights, brooches and such have been "transformed" into hatpin heads. Actually, the genuine Satsuma-ware hatpin usually has a molded flange which is part of the design. Into this flange (or "finding"), is inserted a pin-stem. Other types have a metal sleeve into which the porcelain is mounted, button-fashion, and then a tiny tubular finding is specifically joined to the metallic sleeve to accept the pin-shank.

Hatpin heads changed in design from the popular Victorian hilt-headed pins with their 2″ or 3″ stone-studded and filigree swords, to an almost limitless variety offered through catalogues, in millinery shops, and over the jewelry counters.

Sears, Roebuck and Co., had more than a dozen assorted hatpins in their Fall 1903 "wish book", including a "patented novelty" of an imitation pearl hatpin "made of metal but lustred and unbreakable". Evidently the "novelty" wore off, because even at the low cost of 5¢ each, this type was not advertised in subsequent catalogues.

Most hatpins advertised in Sears' catalogues, appeared in either the jewelry pages or under "hat accessories". The latter included ribbons, plumes, flowers, and "specialty 7″ or 8″ hatpins", made up "three on a card", and priced to sell from 14¢ to 27¢ per card.

The expensive hand-wrought hatpins made by jewelers catering to an exclusive trade, were a departure from the commonplace but not characterless celluloid or "French Ivory" hatpins sold in "general stores" and later in the "five and dime" established in 1879 by F.W. Woolworth.

Although many pressed pattern glass hatpin heads are of American manufacture -- notably Carnival iridescent glass -- the greater quantity and variety of glass baubles came from Bohemia. Many art glass pieces originated in France and Italy.

The jewelry manufacturing centers in America competed with metallic designs from England, France, and Germany, with the largest quantity of sterling hatpins coming from Britain.

Molded and hand-cut imitations of oriental carvings in faux coral, ivory, and jade, and other simulations of amber and onyx, produced exciting results in color, texture and design. Imitations and substitutes for the real gem or gemstone, were socially accepted by the masses for whom these pieces were produced in the fad or fashion of the day. And hatpins were no exception to that rule.

When we think of plastics, we think today of man-made materials concocted from the chemist's tubes in scientific laboratories. Since much of the "plastics" were made in the latter 19th century during the heady height of the period hatpin, it's not surprising that many of the ornamental heads of hatpins produced from 1890-1925, should have been molded heads of celluloid. These were manufactured as early as 1868 by the Hyatt Brothers, Newark, New Jersey.

"Celluloid" was first used as synthetic ivory in the manufacture of billiard balls. Just as early fashions were late in arriving from Europe to America, so was the use of American-made fashion innovations postponed or slowly accepted on the Continent. This may explain why hatpin heads contrived of plastics imitating ivory, amber, mother-of-pearl, and tortoise shell, were not in vogue until late Victorian times in Britain. This fact is bewildering when one considers that before the early 1900's, the U.S. Patent Office issued over 1,500 patents for various plastic processes.

Still, the Victorians of England and La Modes of France, did not find plastic imitations favorable until the late 1890-1900, when plastic played a valuable part in innovative Art Nouveau jewelry, buttons, and accessories. However, plastic hatpin heads reached their zenith during the Art Deco period rather than in the Art Nouveau era.

The peddler, the town merchant, the catalogues, and the city department stores (with their impressive jewelry counters), each had a proper place within growing America.

It's doubtful that they really competed with one another, for the peddler more likely carried for sale only the cheapest ordinary shoe-button type glass hatpins; the town merchant or milliner catered to neighborhood tastes; the catalogues wooed both taste and pocketbook of those residing in remote places; and the lady in town patronized places which by mere circumstance of location within a "metropolis", offered the "latest from Paris" to its fashion-conscious clientele.

The peddler's simple shoe-button type black or white glassheaded hatpin differed much from the extravagant hatpins offered over the jewelry counters. Such a lovely pin is described by Margaret Page Hood in her novel, *The Sin Mark:*

*". . . Her best hat with its limp ostrich plume, skewered to her pug by a lethal hatpin with a painted china head, rode nor' -by-east . . ."*

Just such a "china head" was often claw-set, similar to mountings used for gemstones in which tiny claws hold down the flat surfaces of the cut gem.

Several china or porcelain heads are more securely and artistically mounted in a bezel setting so that the top scarcely appears above the level of the surrounding metal.

There seems to be no effort made in the above setting to make the ornamental head appear larger as is done in an "illusion" setting. Here the metal, be it only brass instead of precious ore, has its edges shaped so they appear to be part of the gem, thus aggrandizing the actual size of the stone.

Many other innovations were taking place in the pin-stem itself. A good example is the advertisement which appeared in the May 1906, *Woman's Home Companion:*

"The New Revolving Spiral Hat Pin will hold your hat comfortably. Ask at hatpin counter or send 25¢ for handsome new design to Koy-Lo Co., 11 Broadway, New York."

It seems that once the new burst of freedom in design descended upon turn-of-the-century fashion, jewelers who once upon a time used pagan or religious symbols and conservatively limited the gemstones to those of significance and superstition, now turned for inspiration to the Italian Renaissance and sought to reflect the art of that period. Jewelry became not only decorative and/or symbolic, but functional. And hatpins were not orphaned in this use of symbolism.

The bezoar, for instance, was set as a jewel because it was thought to be an antidote against poison; diamonds as victory over enemies; heliotropes for long life; sapphires for escape from danger; topaz to prevent harm; and turquoises for prosperity.

Both gems and their imitations in glass were set with claws or in coronets with open backs so as to expose the stones to light from both behind the mounting and front, with an effect that was almost blinding. The foil "gimmick" was also introduced and was widely used in the manufacture of hatpins which had become the most functional and decorative jewelry items next to, perhaps, the brooch. The latter had already become less functional with the introduction of the safety-pin, needle and thread, snaps and hooks 'n-eyes, and such other devices to make the word "pinning" almost obsolete. While the brooch was delegated to the decorative class of artifices, the hatpin remained both functional and ornamental until the years following World War I. Preceding that time, the hatpin had already entered the legal and historical arenas.

Hatpins with gemstones of lapis-lazuli or sapphire were favored by women because these and other blue stones were emblems of chastity; no doubt the women who fought for prohibition, favored the amethyst because it was supposed to counteract the effects of alcohol -- the amethyst's name signifying the "sobering" gem.

In both design and appearance, the decorative hair pin and hatpin are definitely related; the hatpin differs only after 1832, when the manufactured pin's length and the thick-gauged wire made it quite different from the hairpin of yesteryear. The hand-wrought ornamental hairpins also differed from the machine-made decorative hairpins.

The American suppliers of "raw pins", (without the hatpin head ornament), included: Oakville Company, Oakville, Conn.;

W.R. Cobb Company, Cranston, R.I.; Geo. H. Fuller Company, Pawtucket, R.I.; and F.H. Noble Company, Chicago, Illinois.

The finished products were made by the Providence, Rhode Island companies: Brown & Mills, Waite Thresher, Robert Barton, T.W. Foster, and S. & B. Lederer. The Brewster Co., Attleboro, Mass., also plated the raw pins and then distributed them to jewelers who supplied the myriad of ornamental heads which were joined by a series of various findings to the opposite end of the pointed pin.

England and Germany also supplied pin-shanks of different sizes; some made of steel which was either tempered or left in its "white" or "silver" appearance. Other pins were made of nickel or gilded metal. Morris and Yeomans, Abe Morral Co., and Hiskins & Others, were manufacturers and inventors of various patented designs for the "improvement" of pin-shanks which were guaranteed not to slip from "moorings", and "no more marred millinery".

Hatpins were definitely classed with jewelry items and were ordered from the jewelry sections of catalogues and brochures. They were not considered household items such as needles and pins. Unfortunately, many of the magnificent hatpins which probably represented the epitome in hatpin-art, have been lost as hatpins. The bauble-heads have been guillotined on a jeweler's workbench, the spirit and soul reincarnated into a new "life-style" of ring, brooch, pendant, charm, or trinket.

Period hatpins had become a "way of life", a part of daily living from 1890-1914. Edwin Post, in his book about his famous mother, titled: *Truly Emily Post*, tells how Emily ". . .perched high on a cushion, starchily shirtwaisted, with a broad-brimmed sailor made fast to her hair with pins and a spotted veil, drove the smart cob . . . with great enjoyment to herself and others". Later on, Mrs. Post would climb down from her short-legged stocky horse with its fancy gait and climb up into the newfangled horse-powered motorcar.

In Emlyn Williams' autobiography, *George*, he tells how he sat through a sermon, " . . . the test of endurance. I trained myself not to watch the clock for five minutes on end, for it watched it never moved; then, staring at the woman's hat in front, I tried to imagine her at home before the glass, settling it and spearing it, but I could not; she had sat there always". The date: Dec. 1894, at the height of hatpin days.

And in Ralph G. Martin's *Jennie: The Life of Lady Randolph Churchill*, a footnote reads: "Also fashionable then were the wide-brimmed picture hats that seemed to float on the top of the head and were called hatpin heads, (1895). Women skaters, however, had to be warned how to fall properly -- falling on your back can drive your hatpin into your head".

Finally, from the *Young Ladies Journal*, Jan. 1890: "Hatpins are very fashionable at present, and are worn in every variety of form; they are sometimes of silver, gold, pearl, often very richly jeweled, others are of cut jet, garnets, or oxidized silver. In fact they are seen in every possible form".

Some of the later period hatpins had "guards" or "nibs" that were especially designed and manufactured for use on the extremely long hatpins. The "nibs" became necessary because hatpin-points had proven dangerous to passersby and perhaps to gentlemen callers also. If the suitor tarried too long, he may have feared not the rebuke as much as those sharp points as he leaned over to whisper "sweet nothings" into her ear. It has been suggested that period hatpins were the best chaperones possible, and now we can understand why, for just as the cumbersome corset must have saved many a maiden's virtue, (by giving her time to "reconsider her stay"), so the huge hats with their long, sharp hatpins must have been a barbed-wire barrier against certain advances.

Unfortunately for the hatpin collector and for those seeking prize acquisitions for musems, too many of the choice hatpins have or are being converted into other pieces of fine jewelry without retaining a hint of their former heritage or artistic usefulness.

Although quantities of hatpins were not of solid gold or silver, (since they were manufactured for the masses and were acquired by the thousands), hatpins of "baser metals" were still treated by their makers with much artistic merit. Some of the inferior metals show details of much attention given by ingenious workmen, the same attention paid to counterparts made in precious ore.

In many cases where high relief was required, the design was executed in bronze, the reddish color of the metal providing a particularly well-suited base for gilding. Gilding was an excellent method of obtaining a very rich and simulated effect of enduring gold. Burnished metals also enhanced the overall attraction.

Strangely enough, the most difficult part of the hatpin to correctly plate with silver or gold, is the pin or shaft, for there are no flat surfaces for metal coating to adhere to; rather the pin is a continual cylinder from which the plating material slips and slides. The process for plating the pin-shank or shaft, is both an interesting and amazing technique.

The period hatpins of 1850-1925 production, really outclassed all previous sources of inspiration for jewelry in its numerous forms. This was because hatpin-art had not only ancient art and the art of all ages to be copied, but also that most glorious inspiration for ornamentation carried over by the Renaissance. This heritage was not lost to the artisans of the Victorian, Edwardian, and Art Nouveau periods, and the jewelry -- including hatpins -- of the latter period produced some of the most highly prized pieces for collectors and for museum acquisitions.

Inspiration, scientific discoveries, and inventive genius combined and merged and generated generations of fabricators who contrived, originated, and designed masterful jewelry decorations. The period hatpin is an unusual by-product of all this, a device or contrivance which combined artistic merit, commercial enterprise, and utilitarian purpose.

It would seem that the period hatpin is gone forever, except for the pricking of memory by John Canaday's special report to the *New York Times*: [Dateline, Osaka, Japan, March 15, 1970] -- ". . . but the ugliest thing at the fair, and one of the ugliest anywhere ever, is the monster sponsored by the Fuji Group, a combine of 36 of Japan's major companies. The Fuji Pavillion's enormous pneumatic sausage walls, plus numerous growths and excrescences of inflated plastics throughout the fair, give you the feeling that if you don't like the looks of the world of the future, the most effective weapon against it would be an old-fashioned hatpin".

THE HATPIN IS DEAD! LONG LIVE THE HATPIN!

- - - - -

# CHAPTER IV
## PERIOD HATPINS: HOW TO RECOGNIZE & AVOID FAKED HATPINS

There has been much altering and manipulation of hatpins so as to make such counterfeiting appear to be the genuine article. There are also reproductions marketed under misleading advertising banners, such as "uncirculated" or "old-tyme" hatpins.

As the fascination for yesteryear artifacts increases, the interest in hatpins of 1850-1925, attracts more and more collectors. The desire for hatpins and related objects is now favored with an upward trend, and it's part of the collecting game that a few unscrupulous persons will prey upon the public. This is particularly true when the buying public has been provided with little or no information regarding the period hatpin and its complementary accessories. It's no wonder, then, that so many hatpin "fakes" are being manufactured from old brooches, buttons, modern dress pins, and costume jewelry. Serious study can teach how to recognize such contrivances.

Seldom has the author found deviations from the typical manner in which the hatpin head (the ornament), is mounted or attached to the pin-shank or shaft. A pin is inserted into the center socket or patch, which is known as a jeweler's finding. A tubular or funnel-shaped finding is centerd or added to a "bridge", "arc", or "span", which has been utilized to balance larger and/or heavier ornamental heads to the pin-shank.

Some hatpin heads are custom fitted into a patch or sleeve-type mounting which is usually part of the device or design of the ornamental head.

A small round or tubular piece -- the finding -- is crimped to the pin and serves as a "finishing join" to neatly cover where the ornament and pin are anchored together. This tiny finding securely fastens the bauble to the pinshank. If this small connector is missing from between the ornament and the shaft, chances are the hatpin has either been repaired, is a "home-made" construction, or is simply a contrived hatpin made to fool the unwary collector.

There should be no visible adhesive on a genuine hatpin unless the hatpin has been recently repaired. Hestitate to buy any repaired pin unless it was one which had been damaged in your own handling; or if all the findings are complete and intact, it is possible the pin-shank had been loosened, or shortened, or replaced.

Since many antique buttons and brooches have metallic backings, it would not be difficult for a "forger" to solder silver, ordinary lead, or tin to collectible buttons, brooches, buckles, etc., -- add a long pin-shank -- and it can then "pass" as a "genuine" period hatpin. Unfortunately, this is the case when the collector or dealer has untrained or uneducated eyes.

The rare exception to the above rule regarding metallic adhesives, is the "handmade" ornamental heads which have been converted into hatpins, such as mementoes or souvenirs. However, military buttons and coins are typical examples of hatpins that were manufactured as specialties, and in most cases, the pin was inserted without the use of unsightly adhesives or with the aid of findings. The pin is incorporated rather than merely added to the assemblage. The "finding" can even be an integral part of the design or made a part of the actual mounting.

Seldom are decorative stones merely glued into a mounting. Such stones are set into many types of mountings, such as "claw", "crown", "pave'", "bezel", etc.

Authentic period hatpins had pin-shanks made of tempered steel, brass, nickle, japanned metal, and base metals which were gilded in silver or gold. Pins were also made of gold carat or sterling silver. There were no stainless steel pins used before the first quarter of the 20th century, and tin, copper, and pewter were not utilized as pin-shanks. Be wary of newly manufactured stainless steel pin-shanks.

Antique-type jewelry and reproductions of buttons and brooches are being soldered to a long pin after the shaft has pierced through into the underside of the item being attached. Another method of faking hatpins is to remove the pinning device from a handsome brooch and attach the brooch to a genuine hatpin mounting with its familiar arc or span. This "bridge" reaches the distance across the back of the brooch; solder is then used to cover the two places where the original brooch closure or clasp had been. Some sellers will explain that the "hatpin" has been repaired or "reinforced ", and gives further assurance that the item is an "original". True, the brooch may be antique and collectible, but it is not an original hatpin ornament. Unhappily, there are many such fakes flooding the market.

As with all antiques and collectibles, there will be those who try to pass off articles as "the real McCoy"; but by and large it has been this writer's experience that most antique dealers are reliable. Oftentimes, it is the dealer who has been duped by individuals who have manufactured fake hatpins for a profit.

It's distressing to discover more and more of these fakes even at some of our most reputable establishments and at popular antique shows and sales. But as previously stated, most sellers have been victimized themselves. After all, there have been few "guidelines" for them to follow, and dealers in antiques and collectibles cannot possibly know everything about everything. Whenever the opportunity has presented itself, this writer has tried to educate collectors and buyers on the subject of "fakes". And it is the purpose of this handbook to further such education.

From several sources, the author has learned that a gentleman bought up the once plentiful plain old black or white shoe-button type hatpins with their 8″-12″ pin-shanks. Then, breaking off the small glass marble with a hammer, the preserved pin-shanks of tempered steel are then used in conjunction with old buttons and brooches, thus converting them into "old" hatpins.

Sometimes these longer pins are used to replace shorter pins on genuine hatpins, in order to increase the selling price. Hatpins with the longest pins seem to be the most collectible and therefore bring higher prices.

In the case of the transfer or exchange of pin-lengths, the thing to look for is the difference in color between the ornamental head, or its mounting of gold or silver color. It is unusual to find a tempered steel (bluish-grey) pin on gold or silver heads. Well-crafted ornamental heads of silver, for instance, rarely are mounted on to pins used for those common black and/or white shoe-button type hatpins. Therefore, beware of the inconsistancy of a gilt-headed pin mounted on anything other than a gilt, brass or gold hatpin head. The majority of pin-shanks are nickel plated or a silver color; those with genuine stones in the ornamental heads, are usually mounted on pins that are gold plated or have been gilded.

Upon close scrutiny, most collectors can see how "fakes" are accomplished; therefore, buyers are urged to always carry a magnifying glass to examine the pins and mountings very carefully. Some of these "fakes" are quite beautiful, for the buttons, brooches, and buckles of the period were lovely and the nouveau especially enchanting. And it is true that authentic hatpins of yesteryear can be found with similar designs as those used on buttons and brooches. This is not strange inasmuch as hatpin heads were designed by the same jewelers who created other items of jewelry and decorative ware.

Some hatpins made with a glass bead, brilliant, or faceted bauble of glass, were manufactured with just a small round or funnel-shaped fitting that was attached to the pin-shank by mere insertion into that bushing. Once in a great while, the pin-shank is found imbedded into a small hole made by a drill and then glued for permanence. Some glass heads are fitted into a metallic sleeve.

If the glue is crusty or yellow-looking, chances are it's an authentic hatpin with its "finding" lost. But beware the newer non-smear transparent adhesives of today which were not available during the hatpin era. If you do find a handsome hatpin with a "crusty" adhesive glue, it's likely to be a home-made repair job rather than the work of a fine jeweler. A jeweler of the hatpin era would have taken great pains to repair the hatpin properly, by using the required "finding" to complete the job. All findings are part of the "common stock" items of the jewelry trade.

Be cautioned against purchasing silver-colored metal hatpins as silver unless they are hallmarked "sterling", or have the word "sterling", or "sterling front" stamped into the metal.

Gold and gold-filled hatpins are usually marked "karat", if made in America. (But not all are so marked.) If the pin is gilt, (gold color or gold plated), it is not usually marked. European hatpins are not marked "karat", but "carat"; numerals are an equivalent, i.e., $500 = 14K$ and $750 = 18K$.

Although some gemstones are set in non-precious ore, genuine gems such as diamonds, sapphires, rubies and emeralds are likely never to be set in other than precious ore.

As a general rule, period hatpins of precious ore would be marked as to gold or silver content, since it was a legal requirement to do so, and was a recognized practice by members of the jewelry trade.

Some gold or silver hatpins have pins of matching color -- either plated, rolled gold, or when silver is gilded, vermeil. Gold filled pin-shanks are usually so marked. It's logical to be suspicious of a 14K bauble on a silver-color steel pin; nor is it ordinarily acceptable to find a hallmarked sterling hatpin mounted on a tempered steel or japanned pin-shank. There are exceptions, and there is no doubt that some hatpins with ornaments of precious ore and gems may be found mounted on pins of steel, nickle, or brass. But not likely.

A trick exercised by downright frauds, is the use of old-fashioned metallic or bone collar buttons as "findings". How's the trick accomplished?

A small hole is drilled into the smaller end of the collar button, and the slightly convex side is adhered to a large ornament that was previously manufactured as a button, belt-buckle, clasp, clip, earring, or any number of other wearables.

Although the old-fashioned collar button looks like the shape of an authentic finding properly used on hatpins, the collar button can be detected because of its larger size and its contrast of color compared to the ornament. Once you are familiar with this "fake", it is readily spotted as such. If you are unfamiliar with a man's old-fashioned collar-button, it will be profitable for you to search one out in an antique shop and make a mental note of same.

An advance collector will avoid any hatpin that's been repaired or has evidence of soldering material.

The best final advice is to make your purchases from a reputable dealer, combining his and your store of knowledge and experience on the subject, in conjunction with the information offered in this handbook. If purchasing from a private party, remember the ever-wise admonition: "When in doubt, do without!"

- - - - -

## CHAPTER V

## HATPIN HOLDERS: INCLUDING LOOK-ALIKES & REPRODUCTIONS

*". . .upon lace doilies placed to save the beautiful rosewood top, lay a silver toilet set more magnificent than any Sara had ever seen. The mirror had a long slender handle. Even the glass hatpin case had a silver top."* [The Trembling Hills, by Phyllis A. Whitney]

There are almost as many varieties of hatpin holders as there are hatpins, and like hatpins the holders were made of many materials: silver, gold, copper, crystal and all the glass and porcelains of the period. The most popular type seems to have been the china hatpin holders, for these are the holders which are most plentiful today.

Unfortunately, china hatpin holders are also the most common reproductions sold as authentic period pieces. In addition to reproductions, the "look-alikes", such as the muffineer, salt cellar, sugar-shaker, and pounce pot often deceive both buyer and seller alike.

So little has been detailed regarding the unique hatpin holder, no wonder there's much confusion.

A good way to judge whether or not you are looking at the "look-alike" china muffineer is to examine the shape and size. Muffineers are plump around the middle, plump enough to hold at least a cup or more of sugar. Muffineers have fewer and somewhat irregular-sized holes; as a rule, they have an oval or raised dome. Lastly, if the hole in the base is either dime-sized or smaller, chances are it's not a muffineer but a hatpin holder. Condiment holders usually have a larger cork-hole set in a deep well which worked to catch the excess flow of sugar or spiced seasonings, as the container is filled.

Thus, a sugar-shaker, salt shaker, or muffineer, would not have a flat base but rather a cave-like bottom with a cork-hole in the center.

An article recently stated that many hatpin holders were made of wood. From the description, the wooden product is another "look-alike", namely the pounce pot or sander.

The pounce pot usually measures from 2½″ to 4″ tall, and was used to shake pounce, a finely ground black sand. The sanding process was utilized in the 18th and 19th century as an aid in blotting glazed paper or for creating a more suitable writing surface.

Because pounce pots have covered bases and holes in the top, they could easily be mistaken for hatpin holders. Wooden pounce pots were hollowed out at the bottom, filled with pounce, then plugged and sealed with the bases covered with fabric or paper. Sometimes this paper contained advertising slogans. When the sand was gone, being used up, the pounce pots made of inexpensive wood, were simply discarded and a new one purchased. But one sure clue is the barrel-shape and the exceedingly deep recessed top with its definite bowl-shape. In addition, once empty, most wooden pounce pots are too lightweight to remain upright when hatpins are inserted into the outer-edge holes.

The author's collection of hatpin holders contains a few

unusual examples of china holders which have china tops with pinholes, but the base is only an outer edge of porcelain, the center being hollow. One may well wonder how the sharp points of pins were kept from marring the surface of fine wood or marble. It seems that this type of "bottomless" hatpin holder, was kept on a large comb-and-brush tray which provided ample protection from pin scratches.

Manufacturers' marks on hatpin holders clue us to the dating of same in the mid-19th century and early 20th century. Most have European marks which is not unusual since that was the primary source of most china articles, with the less expensive imports coming from the orient.

The holders were manufactured in brilliant cut, pressed, opaline, and carnival glass. Marion T. Hartung, one of the authorities on Carnival Glass, has stated that the term Carnival Glass, ". . .should properly be applied only to colored pressed glass, with iridescense fired on, as made in America between 1900 and 1925".

Hatpin holders were also beautifully executed in silver, pottery, ceramic, and glazed and unglazed porcelain. Many of the china holders were handpainted by Victorian and Edwardian damsels, for china-painting was a favored pastime. The factories also produced handpainted examples, but most were decorated using ceramic transfers embellished with raised designs and enamelled beading, or overlay gilding.

The holders, signed and unsigned, marked and unmarked, may be found footed, flat, round, square, rectangular, oval, or in an innovative shape of a figural. Because some countries of origin no longer exist, trademarks such as R.S. Prussia, are highly collectible, as are Royal Rudolstadt, and Royal Bayreuth.

Just as it's wrong to generalize that hatpins "came in two standard lengths, nine and twelve inches", so we dare not limit the dimensions of the receptacles which held these pointed objects. The hatpin holders came in every shape and form and were the products of England, France, Germany, Japan, and the many Bohemian provinces of Austria, Prussia, Bavaria, and Czechoslavakia. The hatpin holders from these areas were decorated with flowers, vines, and pastoral scenes, as well as portraits and souvenir issues.

Reed, raffia, straw, metallic thread, and other media were used in the handmade variety called "primitives", which were often hung and displayed from the wood turning or mirror brace of a dresser or vanity table.

Storage for hatpins included silverplated and brass pincushion shoes, fashioned in the styles of footwear worn at the turn-of-the-century. There were also beaded cushions and the especially

56

popular pincushion dolls which were in vogue just prior to and following World War I.

Hatpin holders, molded as a single-piece accomodation for rings, hatpins, and small pins, are hard to come by, being rare and very expensive. The smallest pin holder of this trio on a single mold, was a receptacle for flower pins (sometimes called "violet pins"). Simple straight pins, fan pins, a great variety of jeweled hairpins, and lace pins, were also stored therein. However, some of these pins were double-pronged and usually measured from 3″ to 6″ in length. The ideal storage would have been the open top holders.

The open top hatpin holders were also used for the decorative hairpins which often had a heavy-gauge pin-shank and could therefore not fit into the tiny pin-size holes suited for hatpins. Holders with larger than ¼″ pin-prick holes, were designed to accept this heavier gauge and/or hatpin "nibs" and "protectors".

The large center hole in some hatpin holders has been referred to by some as the "mold opening" from which the piece had been removed from the mold. Some holders have these openings at the bottom, but by and large the majority of hatpin holders have solid bases. The holders with only pin-size holes on top and no hole in the base, probably have an "applied" top or two-mold construction.

Since hats of the 1890-1914 period required the longest hatpins, it seems reasonable to assume that the tallest hatpin holders were produced at that time. After 1832, all hatpin holders were made to lodge the manufactured hatpin. However, since several hatpin holders have been identified by marks as early 19th century in Bavaria and Prussia, it's permissible to assume that bonnet pins with handmade wire pins were worn in the royal courts along with numerous other "conceits" so popular at the time. It's highly unlikely that hatpin holders would have been made before the advent or use of a hatpin. That would be like putting the cart before the horse; that is, unless the holders were made to house other types of decorative pins.

Regardless of speculation, there's no doubt that the greatest quantity of hatpin holders were manufactured with the introduction on the fashion front of period hatpins manufactured in the Machine Age. The dresser set, the commode set, or toilette set, soon required a ring tree, earring hooks, pin tray, and the inevitable hatpin holder. Most hatpin holders were made from 1860-1920, with the later models incorporating little saucers used to keep blouse pins, women's cuff-links, bar pins for women's shirtwaists, and the small hatpin "nibs" or "protectors".

Herman C. Carter, writing about *Milady's Dresser Accessories*, stated: "The elaborate coiffure, the large and sometimes floppy hat, the hatpin, and the hatpin holder came in rapid fire succession. All of this to the great delight of the hair-dresser, milliner, and the makers of ladies dresser sets. It was almost like a conspiracy against the man-of-the-house's pocketbook".

In the *Gentlemen's Magazine*, (1764), we read that the King of Prussia "at great expense" established a porcelain factory and "has already brought it to such perfection as to rival that at Meissen".

Some of the most highly prized -- and priced -- hatpin holders are those marked R.S. Prussia, not to be confused with the more plentiful R.S. Germany mark.

Wherever fuel and earth-clay are readily at hand, the area becomes a natural resource for man's pottery and porcelain factories. The consistencies of clays vary, as do the colors, and the variations lent themselves to identifiable kinds of china being produced by the various makers. The Staffordshire countryside was dotted with pottery and porcelain factories, as was the Thuringian forest in Germany. Of special interest to collectors of hatpin holders, is the factory at Volkstedt-Rudolstadt known as Schaffer & Vater (S&V Mark). The Crown and Sunburst with incised "R", was the mark of this company which was located in the Volkstedt area; the mark is found on some of the most highly collectible Art Nouveau bisque, jasperware, and china hatpin holders. The factory produced from 1890 until it burned to the ground in 1918. The author's conjecture is that the "R" denotes the royal Rudolstadt family which may or may not have been responsible for financing the first kilns in the Thuringian forest.

The S&V mark should not be confused with the fine, delicate china which is marked Royal Rudolstadt.

Porcelain or china holders are usually made in the two or more mold process in which the top of the holder is applied to the base. If the holder has an attached saucer, it would probably be a three-mold unit. All molded pieces are joined by fettling which smoothed the seams of the greenware; then these seams were additionally camouflaged with applied gold decorative rings or beading after firing. This decorative work was done after the first glaze was added; then another firing took place before the final embellishment. If the ceramic or porcelain is unglazed, it is called bisque.

The range of color, style, and design of a hatpin holder is endless, from a delicate porcelain paper-thin example, measuring only 4″ high, to a heavier china hatpin holder 10″ tall which is best used for the long-stemmed hatpin beauties of the turn-of-the-century.

The wealthy could afford commode articles in sterling and gold, but there were the less expensive dresser and toilette sets which included hatpin holders made of stoneware, "French Ivory" (celluloid), and base metals for the more "common trade".

Dresser sets or hatpin holders marked "Nippon", represented the least expensive china imports and until recently were rather snubbed by collectors. However, the articles marked "Nippon", or even the unmarked but obvious oriental works, are some of the loveliest of all and should not carry the "stigma" often attributed to such merchandise. Not until a few years ago have "Nippon" decorated wares gained the respect they deserve. Although "Royal Austria", "Germany", "Bavaria", "Limoges", and other favored marks are considered more valuable in a monetary sense, they oftentimes cannot compete in artistic excellence with the "Nippon".

An excellent book, particularly for identifying marks for NIPPON porcelains, including hatpin holders, is Van Patten's, *The Collector's Encyclopedia of Nippon Porcelain* (Collector Books).

The Nippon period covers from 1858-1921, and the word "Nippon" is Japanese for Japan which translates into "place the sun comes from" or "land of the rising sun". It's hard to believe that no merchandise was shipped to the United States from Japan until 1858. This is the year our government entered into a trade agreement with the Japanese government "at the request of Commodore Perry". Japanese art, imported as "Nippon", first came to our country during the Philadelphia Centennial Exhibition in 1876. Thus, when America celebrated its Bicentennial (1976), it also marked the first 100 years of trade with the Empire of Japan.

After March 1, 1921, the word "Nippon" was ruled unacceptable for "country of origin" for imports from Japan. It is then a simple matter for collectors to date their Japanese hatpin holders because anything produced with the "Made In Japan" marking, was manufactured AFTER 1921.

Although Japanese wares for domestic use were simple in design, those exported to the United States and Europe were copied in the more complicated designs of European art forms. Ironically, while artists and craftsmen in European factories were imitating the oriental motifs, such as Blue Willow and Art Nouveau inspirational motifs, so the Japanese workers were busy copying pastorial scenes such as Dutch Windmills, and Colonial Dames.

Two excellent source books about NIPPON appear in the RECOMMENDED READING section of this handbook.

From 1900-1910, the manufacture of extremely long hatpins was joined by the mass production of hair ornaments, both requiring holders of one kind or another. Varying shapes and sizes of ornaments and hatpin heads were fashioned of shell, amber, bone, hard rubber, horn, and celluloid. Bent celluloid hairpins from 2″ to 4″ were a good example of the transition from wire-made to wonderful science-blended imitations. Such plastics were a return to the ancient art of using natural products manipulated by man for woman. To store the above mentioned pins, holders were manufactured of synthetics, too.

To sum up regarding hatpin holders, their "look-alikes" and "reproductions": as a general rule, hatpin holders have solid bases with from six to twelve pin-holes on top to accept hatpins. Hatpin holders have concave or only slightly domed tops, and seldom have the familiar "steeple" associated with the muffiner or sugar-shaker. If hatpin holders are so shaped, they will not have a cork in the bottom, but have a solid base. The hatpin holder is seldom "plump" in design; if it is, it will also have a solid base.

Some hatpin holders do have applied tops pierced with small pin-holes which circle a dime-sized opening in the top. The base of these types of holders is always solid, with no hole in the bottom. Most mold openings at the bottom of hatpin holders, are either too small to successfully pour in a condiment, or the openings are too large or irregular to accomodate a round cork. Most hatpin holders are altogether too slender to prove practical for use as a condiment holder; or if big and round, have no possible way of filling from outside to inside.

Even some experts in the field have overlooked the possibility that the open-top holders could have been used as a toothbrush holder.

Hairpins and pin-ornaments with heavy pin-shanks could not be housed in tiny pin-holes made for hatpins only. Thus, authentic period hatpin holders can readily be identified as the closed-top receptacle with tiny pin-holes. One thing is for certain: the pin-sized holes in authentic hatpin holders cannot be used for either toothbrushes nor for other articles such as double-pronged hair ornaments, heavy gauge hairpins, nor sheath-type corsage and scarf pins. Some holders have larger than pin-size openings in the tops and these might well have been made for the many other types of pins besides hatpins.

Be wary of a dealer who tries to sell a china pomandour or pomander as a hatpin holder; also any one who produces a covered porcelain dish with small holes in its cover. The latter was actually made to house perfumed soap. Larger covered dishes, without holes in the top, were toothbrush holders. The usual sales-pitch is that hatpins were pushed through the small holes into the soap. This was supposed to keep the pin-shanks "sharp", "upright", and "sweet-smelling". Fiddlesticks and hogwash! That's a soft-soap-sell if there ever was one. And considering there was no stainless steel made during the period, what about rusty pin-shanks?

Hatpin holders with attached trays, in various designs, are

being reproduced in Japan. Made for export to the U.S.A., they are sold from $2.40-$3.95 retail, and are unpainted blanks. Each reproduction is made by a different Japanese firm and are currently being imported by American companies dealing with persons who buy for resale to collectors.

The china "blanks" are imported, sold, and then handpainted by today's enterprising women attending the china painting classes which have become almost as popular as those held in the Victorian days. Some of the finished products are for personal use; others are sold to antique shops or at shows. Some are marked as "reproduction" or "new"; others are passed off as the "old", "authentic" hatpin holders of an earlier period.

All of the aforementioned reproductions imported as "blanks", have paper labels which are easily removed. The holders then have no identifying marks as to country of origin or manufacture. Once in a while an artist's punch mark may be seen, but no identification of country, quality of ore, or date of piece.

Veracious vendors of antiques and collectibles will tag such merchandise as "reproduction"; unfortunately, all sellers are not honest nor do they feel a responsibility to their trade. Unless you are buying from a reputable dealer who knows her inventory, it's suggested that the hatpin holder collector purchase only imprinted or incised, trademarked merchandise.

New plaster-of-Paris molds are being created and produce entirely new hatpin holders that were never manufactured in the vintage hatpin era (1850-1930). The demand for hatpin holders has increased, and with so many novice collectors ready to buy any piece with holes in the top and a solid bottom, all collectors must be all the more cautious when purchasing hatpin holders without a mark under the glaze, or a china piece that lacks the "feel" of fine old porcelain pieces.

Regretably, there are marked reproductions being newly produced in England and offered for sale at gift marts across the country. Reproductions of both "Moss Rose" and "Romantic" patterns are being offered for sale in the wholesale market. It would again be up to antique dealers as to whether to represent the merchandise for what it is.

The "flow-blue" Romantic patterns and the scenic Moss Rose, are clearly marked on the bottom: Staffordshire, England. However, the authentic old pieces from which these have been reproduced, also show the manufacturer's trademark which is a lion and unicorn. The word "ironstone" is also imprinted. The new hatpin holders in the Romantic pattern are marked: "flow blue", a recent term used by collectors referring to "old" china. It is now being coined by the company which is reproducing the old patterns.

61

The new English reproductions are wholesaled at $4.50 (painted), but have been retailing from $12.50 to $35.00 -- or whatever the trade will bear.

Now there's nothing wrong in buying beautifully executed reproductions of popular items, and the hatpin holder is coming into its own because of the demand and interest in yesteryear collectibles. What is highly objectionable, is the fraudulent intent in selling such items as original or old. The unpardonable is their sale as genuine antiques.

Ceramic decals with a slight variation from the original trademark for R.S. Prussia (Red Mark), are being fired on to reproduction hatpin holders and stickpin holders, and are then passed off as "collectible" R.S. Prussia china. Some of the very finest porcelains came from Prussia; the reproduction of hatpin holders and stickpin holders represent the worst quality of a heavy ironstone.

A collector is often willing to pay a disproportionate share of the selling price of a complete or partially complete dresser set for the single item -- the hatpin holder. Is it a wonder, then, that so many toilette sets have that important piece missing!

Some of the most imaginative holders were created during the Victorian era. Whatever the excesses of Victorian ornamentation, they at least grasped the meaning and mastery of "decoration" in its most lavish sense, utilizing to the utmost the principle of contrast in form and fantasy. It seems the Victorian could be both decorative and functional at one and the same time, something we "moderns" are not able to achieve very often in either our square skyscrapers nor in our space-age furniture -- not to mention the cold restraint used in the newer concepts of jewelry and art. Whatever we have that's warm and "free-wheeling", comes from reproductions of work achieved in bygone eras, with particular emphasis today on Art Nouveau and Art Deco.

Hatpin holders are a unique collection in themselves and some collectors eagerly buy them without special interest in the hatpins for which the holders were made. A collection of holders can grow out of the simple necessity of storing a treasury of hatpins -- or vice-versa.

In Isabella Mary Beeton's, *The Book of Household Management*, there's a splendid line that's an apt description for the hatpin and hatpin holder: "A place for everything and everything in its place."

Surely her 1861 publication points to hatpins and hatpin holders!

- - - - -

# SECTION II.

## CHAPTER I
COLOR PLATES

## CHAPTER II
BLACK & WHITE PLATES

## CHAPTER III
DRAWINGS & ILLUSTRATIONS

# PLATE 1

Satsuma ware is a hard glazed yellow-beige porcelain made in the former province of Satsuma, in Kiushu, one of the Japanese Islands. Each piece is highly decorated with gold tracings. When viewed under magnification, the glaze appears crackled, and the handpainted miniatures are technically perfect in brushstroke and overall execution of design. Many hatpins were exported in pairs, packed in thinly cut wooden boxes to accomodate 12″ to 14″ overall lengths. The metallic cup findings usually meet the decorative trim, such as beading or colored banding. The flat disc findings are sometimes called "sleeves", and are similar to the kind used on buttons. The ball-type or flat variations, usually have one-of-a-kind motifs. Satsuma ware hatpins depicting oriental figures or portraits are most desirable.

Satsuma Hatpins for export are circa 1905. (Collection: Doris Gaston)

**Row & No.**          **Description**

Row 1, 1. 1¾″ handpainted Satsuma on 10¼″ steel pin. Two silk kimona-clad Japanese women. Heavy gold beading. [Metallic mount missing]

Row 1, 2. 1½″ handpainted Satsuma on 8¾″ steel pin. Pair of Robin Redbreasts among raised enamelled blossoms. [Note how metallic cup mounting meets the trim, and how the tubular finding is crimped to the pin-shank.]

Row 2, 1. 1¾″ handpainted floral Satsuma on 10″ steel pin.

Row 2, 2. 1¼″ round handpainted Satsuma set into a cup finding. 9¾″ japanned pin. Wisteria and Lilies in exquisite detail.

Row 2, 3. 1¾″ handpainted Satsuma on 7¼″ steel pin. (Note metallic mounting has been lost and the unpainted porcelain is exposed.) Iris blooms in profusion; a favorite subject matter of Japanese artists.

Row 3, 1. 1¾″ handpainted Satsuma on 10¾″ steel pin. Wisteria motif, with heavy gold beading and overlay.

Row 3, 2. 1″ round Satsuma hatpins; detailed Dragon in gold and cinnabar coloring. 8¼″ unusual gilt patch mounting and brass pin-shank.

Row 3, 3. 1½″ Satsuma, handpainted birds and leaf motif. 10½″ steel pin.

**PLATE 2**

(Collection: Doris Gaston, unless otherwise noted.)

**Row & No.**                                    **Description**

Row 1, 1. 1¾" handpainted porcelain with heavy gold overlay. 7½" gilt
pin is attached to ornamental head with decorative baroque
sleeve which is cupped into typical porcelain-type jewelers' finding. Victorian motif, circa 1890.

Row 1, 2. 2½" openwork, gilt over brass, art nouveau mounting for an
emerald-cut faceted amythest glass stone, bezel-set on each
side. 10" gilt pin. Circa 1900.

Row 1, 3. 2¼" rare cased mercury glass head, crimped tubular finding
attached to typical cup-type receptacle for free-form glass
heads. Probably Bohemian glass. Circa 1905.

Row 2, 1. 1¼" art nouveau floral mounting for escutcheon. Gilt over
brass, the gold escutcheon plate is rimmed with granular
beading and inscribed, "Lulu". 8" steel pin. Circa 1905.

Row 2, 2. 1½" gilt over brass early nouveau mounting for 3/8" bezel-
set, faceted, pink glass. 7¾" steel pin. Circa 1890.

Row 2, 3. ¾" gold ornament accented with small cabachon-cut Persian
turquoise. 7" gilt pin. Victorian, circa 1880.

Row 2, 4. 1¾" unusual filigree oxidized brass mounting for gold escutcheon engraved with monogram. Etruscan influence in
Aesthetic and Victorian periods. 7¾" steel pin. Circa 1880.

Row 3, 1. ½" overall head comprised of cabachon-cut amythest bezel-
set with a faceted crystal separator in gold mounting joined
to 5½" gilt pin. Design attributed to Tiffany, circa 1890. Often
boxed in pairs, with matching veil or hairpins, these exquisite
hatpins usually have cabachon-cut stones with crystal, topaz,
or amythest separators and diversified gold mountings. (See
hatpin, Row 3, 5., for variation in design.)

Row 3, 2. 5/8" gilt over brass art nouveau mounting for two genuine
polished free-form amythests, on 8" steel pin. Circa 1905.
[Collection: Barbara Hammell]

Row 3, 3. ¾" gilt over brass pierced mounting for a bezel-set many-
faceted oval amythest color stone set atop 8" steel pin-shank.
Victorian vintage, circa 1890. [Collection: Barbara Hammell]

Row 3, 4. 1½" baroque Mother-of-Pearl hand-set into engraved custom-
made, rolled gold strap type mounting. Faceted ruby-color
glass accent. 6" steel pin. This is a favorite souvenir of visits
to seashore resorts, but more elaborate than most hatpins
which are comprised of small shells entwined in gold wire.
Circa 1890. [Collection: Barbara Hammell]

Row 3, 5. 1" overall head, with cabachon-cut garnet atop 5½" gilt pin.
[See comments, Row 3, 1.]

**PLATE 3**

(Collection: Doris Gaston)

| Row & No. | Description |
| --- | --- |

**Row & No.**  **Description**

Row1, 1. 1″ marked "sterling", art nouveau stylized woman, w/fine repousse' work. 8¾″ steel pin. Probably American manufacture, circa 1905.

Row 1, 2. 2¾″ Aesthetic period or Arts and Crafts designed head, marked "sterling". Hollow silver, atop 8″ steel pin. Circa 1885.

Row 1, 3. 2 7/8″ baroque design, braiding and silver granular work. Marked "sterling"; monogram "D", dated '66 [1866]. Bezel-set, faceted amythest on 10″ japanned pin.

Row 1, 4. 2¼″ marked "sterling" head, lightly etched and engraved hollow-ware. Aesthetic period, or Arts and Crafts, circa 1885. 8″ steel pin.

Row 1, 5. 1½″ high art nouveau stylized silver color mounting comprised of calla lilies, forming a unique lodging for a 1¼″ pearlized drop. Unmarked metallic content and unsigned. 8¼″ brass pin. Circa 1905.

Row 2, 1. 1″ art nouveau figural woman with flowing hair comprising entire ornamental head, placed atop 6¾″ brass pin. Ornament is marked "sterling". Circa 1900.

Row 2, 2. 1¼″ x 1½″ comedic baroque figural, hollow silver. 7¼″ pin-shank stamped "sterling top". High repousse' work. Circa 1880.

Row 2, 3. ¾″ x 1″ woman's portrait from Aesthetic or Arts and Crafts period. 8″ pin-shank, stamped "sterling top". Circa 1880.

Row 3, 1. ¾″ figural hand-wrought sterling Dutch shoe. Netherland's hallmark, circa 1900. 7¾″ steel pin.

Row 3, 2. 1¼″ hollow, etched and engraved head with a floral finding marked "sterling". 9″ oxidized pin. Circa 1870.

Row 3, 3. 7/8″ high art nouveau woman's head serves as a mounting for a monogrammed escutcheon. Marked "925 sterling". 7½″ steel pin. Circa 1905.

Row 3, 4. 1¼″ sterling figural floral sweet pea, mounted on 8″ steel shank stamped with trademark, "Delamothe". Circa 1900.

**PLATE 4**
(Collection: Doris Gaston)

| Row & No. | Description |
| --- | --- |

Row 1, 1. 3″ oxidized brass, highly stylized Art Nouveau four-panel head, each accented with a 1/8″ bezel-set amythest color brilliant. A ¼″ amythest color accent is utilized as an artistic closure for the pierced panels. 9½″ brass pin joined to head with tubular and floral jewelers' findings. Circa 1910.

Row 1, 2. 2¼″ oxidized silver alloy, grape leaf motif, with 2″ molded amythest glass accent embellishing the fruit. Crimped tubular finding attaches ornamental head to 11½″ steel pin. Circa 1900.

Row 1, 3. 2½″ oxidized brass with one 1/8″ pronged amythest color accents in each of the four panels. The bezel-set, ½″ round amythest color stone is further enhanced by four cupped and pronged 1/8″ faceted amythest color brilliants. Circa 1910.

Row 2, 1. 1¼″ x 1¾″ magnificent wire-worked and pierced brass frame mounting for a 1¼″ polished turquoise matrix gemstone. The triangular art nouveau head is accented by applied leaves and three bezel-set cabachon-cut turquoise, with matrix intact. A crimped tubular jewelers' finding attaches ornamental head to 11¼″ brass pin. Circa 1905.

Row 2, 2. 1¼″ x 1¼″ triangular art nouveau oxidized brass head accented by bezel-set ½″ amythest color stone. 9½″ brass pin. Circa 1905.

Row 3, 1. 2″ wire-worked, pierced art nouveau brass frame displays a bezel-set emerald-cut ¾″ faceted amythest color stone. 10″ steel pin. Circa 1905.

Row 3, 2. 1½″ x 2¾″ high art nouveau styles, oxidized brass frame mounting for inner prong-mounted ¾″ matched oval-faceted amythest color stones. 9¾″ brass pin. Circa 1905.

Row 3, 3. ½″ oxidized silver alloy mounting for many faceted ¾″ round amythest color molded glass, ringed by 16 prong-set 1/8″ amythest color brilliants. 7½″ steel pin. Circa 1900. (Crimped tubular and floral findings are similar to the hatpin shown Row 1, 1. above.)

## PLATE 5

(Collection: Doris Gaston)

Art Nouveau variations, circa 1910. Antiqued brass ornamental heads, each hand fastened to a pin-shank with brass tubular or funnel types of jewelers' findings.

| Row & No. | Description |
|---|---|
| Row 1, 1. | 2¾" bezel-set head w/four ¼" topaz-color faceted stones, atop an 11¾" brass pin. |
| Row 1, 2. | 3" bezel-set head, w/two 1/8" and one ¾" oval topaz-color faceted stones, atop a 9¾" brass pin. |
| Row 1, 3. | 3" head, with one round bezel-set 3/8" faceted topaz-color stone, atop a 10" pin. (Note similar designs used on panels of hatpin head No. 1) |
| Row 2, 1. | 2¼" pierced frame, with escutcheon-type mounted bezel-set ½" oval faceted topaz-color stone, atop 10¾" steel pin. |
| Row 2, 2. | 2¾" unusual lariat framed round, bezel-set and faceted 5/8" topaz-color stone, on a 7½" steel pin. |
| Row 3, 1. | 1" x 1¾" pierced frame accented with three rows of approximately 45 1/8" topaz-color, faceted brilliants, prong-set, with ½" bezel-set and faceted stone. Mounted on 9¾" brass pin. |
| Row 3, 2. | 1¼" x 1¾" striking symmetry in a frame accented by mythological head and ¾" oval bezel-set, faceted citrine. 7¾" brass pin. |
| Row 3, 3. | 2" panelled head, accented by florals descending from bezel mounting into which is set a ½" round faceted topaz-color stone. 9¾" brass pin. |

72

**PLATE 6**
(Collection: Doris Gaston)

**Row & No.**                    **Description**

Row 1, 1.  6½" high by 1¾" wide, silver hatpin stand. Art nouveau, highly stylized container custom sized for plush velvet cushion. Four ring or neck-chain holders. Circa 1905.

Row 1, 2.  5½" high by 2¾" stand, with 16 pin-holes. Etched and engraved silver hatpin holder, unmarked. Circa 1880.

Row 2, 1.  4" high by 2¾" wide platform, silver hatpin stand with figural cherub. 1½" plush cushion. Unmarked. Circa 1895.

Row 2, 2.  4½" high with 2½" platform. Thistle-cut amythest color stone. Silver plated, with 1¾" plush cushion. Circa 1900.

Row 3, 1.  ½" x 3" long, figural golf bag hatpin stand. Marked: "sterling 950". Two 1¼" golf putters form the legs for stand. Rare. Circa 1895.

**PLATE 7**
(Collection: Doris Gaston)
**Row & No.**            **Description**

Row 1, 1.  1″ art nouveau head, marked "sterling front". 9¾″ steel pin. Possibly Unger Bros., Newark, N.J. Circa 1903.

Row 1, 2.  ½″ x 1″ Billiken figural hatpin head, marked: "Sterling" with letters PGB in heart-shaped trio of punchmarks. Billiken-shape etched with words "Trade Mark Billiken", as part of entire authentic trademark for this highly collectible hatpin. 7¾″ brass pin. Billikens were considered by many a good luck symbol, and were produced as such in many types of souvenir items and artifacts. A 1909 Billiken Co., Chicago, copyrighted postcard reads:

> "I am the Source of Luckiness,
> Observe my twinkling eyes--
> Success is sure to follow those
> Who keep me closely by."

Row 1, 3.  ½″ x 1″ figural woman's head in suffragette cap. Marked "sterling top", on 7¾″ steel pin. High repousse'. Circa 1900.

Row 2, 1.  1″ art nouveau stylized woman's head. Marked: "sterling top". Woman's hair forms design in relief. 7¼″ steel pin. Circa 1905.

Row 2, 2.  1″ art nouveau finely detailed woman in a half clam shell-shaped background. Marked: "sterling front". 7¾″ steel pin. Circa 1905.

Row 2, 3.  1″ art nouveau head, marked "925 sterling" with Unger Bros. trademark. High repousse'; exquisite detail. 8½″ steel pin. Circa 1903.

Row 3, 1.  1″ full figural Indian head, marked "sterling" with letter "S" in diamond shaped trademark. 7½″ steel pin. Circa 1900.

Row 3, 2.  1½″ silver, enameled head. Oblong trademark symbol: ALFACCA. Design and workmanship suggests Arts and Crafts manufacture for Liberty & Co. 9½″ steel pin. Circa 1890.

Row 3, 3.  ¾″ x 1½″ head, comprised of Naval insignia on escutcheon, marked "sterling", hollow top. 9¾″ steel pin. Circa 1895.

Row 4, 1.  ½″ x 1″ figural man in turban. High repousse' and detailed etching. Marked "sterling" and "sterling top" on patch-type finding which secures ornamental head to a 6¾″ steel pin. Circa 1890.

Row 4, 2.  ½″ x ¾″ art nouveau (miniature rendition of hatpin, Row 2, 2.)

Row 4, 3.  ½″ x 1¼″ figural, high repousse', art nouveau Gibson Girl motif. Marked "sterling top". Circa 1900.

**PLATE 8**
(Collection: Doris Gaston)

| Row & No. | Description |
|---|---|

Top  1½" x 2" curved head w/four ½" pear-shaped bezel-set faceted sapphire color stones, and a 1" oval, bezel-set center stone, all girdled with approximately 60 cupped and pronged 1/8" faceted brilliants. A 1" bridge or curved span and small tubular finding anchors magnificent ornament to an 8" steel pin. The blue faceted glass is of such clarity, it requires no foil backing, refracting its own brilliance. Circa 1895.

Row 2, 1. 1" x 1" overall head, including brass cup with tubular finding anchored to 9¼" brass pin. A round faceted green color stone is bezel-set and circled with fifteen 3/16" foiled and cupped brilliants. Circa 1895.

Row 2, 2. 1¾" triangular ornament with pave'-set, cupped and pronged brilliants. White alloy metallic mounting, crimped with small brass tubular finding to an 11¾" steel pin. Circa 1895.

Center  3¼" rare ornamental head with multi-color and clear pave'-set 1/8" brilliants. The four diamond shapes are positioned with two 1/8" x 3¼" long brass straps on reverse side. A center hole, where strapping crosses and a 9¾" brass pin is thrust, is anchored with a crimped tubular finding. Circa 1910.

Bottom  1¾" brass heart-shaped frame, with filigree wire and individually cupped and pronged brilliants ranging in sizes from 1/16" to 1/8". Six rare crescent-shaped amythest-color pronged stones accent the triangular ½" bezel-set center which is not foiled but refracts light from its many faceted brilliant-cut glass. Circa 1905.

**PLATE 9**

(Collection: Doris Gaston)

**Row & No.**           **Description**

Top        1¼ " iridescent porcelain ball, ceramic transfer with handpainted accents and heavy gold overlay. 8½ " steel pin w/patch finding. Circa 1895.

Row 2, 1.   1 1/8" enamel on sterling, art nouveau floral, crimped tubular finding attached to 11¾ " gilt pin. Circa 1900.

Row 2, 2.   1" art nouveau floral figural, enamelled on copper. Stamped: "G.E.D." on reverse side. 9½ " brass pin. Circa 1900.

Center     1¼ " brass button-type sleeve-mounted porcelain w/ceramic transfer. Maiden with butterfly on her fingertips. 8" steel pin. Subject is typical of Aesthetic and early Arts & Crafts Movement. Circa 1880.

Row 3, 1.   1¼ " handpainted porcelain with full metallic patch and prong mounting. A Victorian pastime was china-painting, including hatpin heads. 6¼ " steel pin. Circa 1885.

Row 3, 2.   1" handpainted porcelain, stud-type set into special pronged mounting with four smaller points bent inward to grasp and secure stud-end of button; four larger outward flaring braces hold the saucer-shaped edge. Small matching stud buttons were used for blouses (called "waists"), with matching collar fastenings. 9¾ " brass pin is joined to unique mounting device by crimping it to the pin-shank with tiny tubular jewelers' finding. Circa 1890.

Row 4, 1.   1" mosaic, set into brass button-sleeve type metallic mounting, w/gold-wire trim. Stamped "GS" on reverse. 8" brass pin. Circa 1875.

Row 4, 2.   1¼ " rare double framed and metallic mounted mosaic with granular trim. 6½ " brass pin. Crica 1875.

Row 4, 3.   1" rare two-piece pierced brass mounted mosaic with braided trim. Intricate detailing and design. (Replacement 10¾ " steel pin, reduces value. Original pin was brass.) Circa 1875.

## PLATE 10
(Collection: Milly Combs)

Peacock Eye glass, when related to hatpins, refers to a handmade Bohemian glass which incorporated the use of silver foil within the glass, with a cobalt-blue glass "dot" representing the pupil of the "eye" in the peacock feather. Art glass hatpin heads refers to the exquisitely handmade varieties other than glass which is not hand done but is either pressed or blown into a mold. Carnival glass, a highly iridescent pressed pattern glass, and blown iridescent glass hatpin heads, are not usually categorized with foiled glass, plique'-a-jour, Tiffany glass, etc. Peacock Eye glass hatpins were made and worn through the Aesthetic Period, Art and Crafts movement, and throughout the Art Nouveau period. It's decline began approximately with the end of World War I, and it is therefore safe to date these hatpins, circa 1905.

| Row & No. | Description |
|---|---|
| Top, 1. | 7½″ steel pin with 7/8″ oval head. |
| Top, 2. | 7 7/8″ steel pin with 11/16″ emerald glass. |
| Top, 3. | 9½″ steel pin with 3 3/8″ horn figural butterfly accented with 99 rose color, pink, yellow, and white rhinestones, and two 3/8″ peacock eyes. |
| Top, 4. | 8″ steel pin with ½″ head, with silver foil glass ball on top half, with peacock eye. |
| Top, 5. | 8 3/16″ steel pin, with 9/16″ head. Silver foil glass, flattened glass globe with a peacock eye each side. |
| Top, 6. | 8″ steel pin with 3/8″ head, with peacock eye. |
| Row 2, 1. | 6 3/8″ steel pin with 5/8″ head. Red foil glass ball with peacock eye on top. |
| Row 2, 2. | 7¾″ steel pin, ½″ head, peacock eye cabachon set into a gilt metallic funnel or conical shaped mounting. |
| Row 2, 3. | 10″ gilt pin, 1″ head, with ½″ round peacock eye cabachon set into a four-sided whiplash openwork design. Gilt over brass. |
| Row 3, 1. | Stickpin with a bezel-set peacock eye. Gilded copper. Stickpins were worn by men and women. They were referred to as "cravat" pins for men, and "scarf" pins for women. |
| Row 3, 2. | 9¼″ steel pin, 3¼″ head. Figural butterfly is pressed horn, with 5/16″ peacock eye accent and 15 rhinestones. |
| Row 3, 3. | 7½″ steel pin, 1″ head, with a four-sided art nouveau floral, each mounted with a 3/16″ bezel-set peacock eye and topped with a 7/16″ peacock eye. |
| Row 3, 4. | 7 7/8″ steel pin, 1 1/16″ head, two-sided gilded brass. Openwork consists of art nouveau inspired scrolls. A 3/8″ peacock eye accents each side of ornamental head. |
| Row 3, 5. | 7½″ steel pin, 1″ overall three-sided leaf motif. Gilded brass with 3/8″ cabachon peacock eye bezel-set atop ornamental head. |
| Row 4, 1. | 4¾″ steel pin, 1″ head, hallmarked: C.H. [Charles Horner]. Hallmarks: Passant Lion [England]; Shield with three "dots" [Chester], Letter G [1907]. Ornament is a shallow convex cabachon peacock eye each side, mounted in a sterling collet setting. This kind of setting is a metal band which embraces the outer edge of the glass or stone in a kind of flange fitting. This is then secured, as in this hatpin, by a bead-shape and a tubular finding crimped to the pin-shank. |
| Row 4, 2. | 6¾″ steel pin, 1¼″ head, gilded art nouveau, with a 3/8″ peacock eye each side, and two blue foil glass cabachons, and a 3/16″ peacock eye on top. |
| Row 4, 3. | 7½″ overall gilt with ball and tubular finding with ½″ hollow tube for insertion of various brooches. Two wire standards support the brooch on each side. Brooch measures 1 1/8″ overall, with a fine filigree mounting, set atop a ring which enhances the 1″ x ½″ cabachon peacock eye. |

**PLATE 11**

(Collection: Milly Combs, unless otherwise noted.)

**Row & No.**                    **Description**

Row 1, 1.   7 3/8″ steel pin, with 1″ ivory hollow-carved head. Chrysanthemum and other floral motifs. Head has threaded tubular finding which unscrews.

Row 1, 2.   7 3/8″ steel pin, with 1 1/8″ figural ivory elephant, hand carved. [Endangered specie]

Row 1, 3.   7″ steel pin, with 1½″ hand carved walrus ivory. Hollow carving depicts walrus, and undulating tidal waves. [Endangered specie]

Row 1, 4.   8½″ steel pin, with 1½″ hand carved full figural ivory elephant balanced on ivory ball. [Collection: Author's]

Row 1, 5.   10″ steel pin, with ¾″ bone, carved in a woven basket weave, cross-hatch design. Japanese bone carving.

**Five Satsuma Hatpins [See PLATE 1]**

Wisteria design, Geshia girls, and the Seven Suns, were some additional motifs found in the exported hatpins from Japan. The round porcelain heads range from 1″ to 2″, on 8½″ to 11¼″ pins; the elongated heads measure from 1¼″ to 2″, usually on 9½″ to 11¼″ pins. Many pin-shanks were shortened when laws required that the tip not protrude from the hat more than 2″ from the brim without a "protector" or "nib". Satsuma "nibs" were exported, but are a rare find. Nibs vary in sizes from ¼″ to ½″, overall.

Pique′ hatpins are rarely found and are highly collectible. Pique′ work is the inlaying of gold and/or silver into genuine tortoise shell. The tiny gold beading is placed to form a design. Gold beading applied in decorative fashion to metal, is called granular work. Note the variance in decoration on the hatpins pictured on this Plate. [Tortoise is endangered specia]

Center        7¾″ steel pin, with 1¼″ tortoise pear-shaped head, with ribboned pique′ work. (Collection: Author's)

Bottom, 1.  6 3/8″ steel pin, with ½″ ball. Tortoise dotted with gold pique′ work in simple overall pattern.

Bottom, 2.  7¼″ steel pin, with 1½″ pear-shaped head of tortoise shell. Much fancy pique′ work.

Bottom, 3.  9″ steel pin, with 1¼″ tortoise ball, and dangling ½″ tortoise ball, both in Roman Gold (pink) pique′ beading and inlaid bands of gold. Rare. (Collection: Author's)

Bottom, 4.  12″ steel pin, 1″ tortoise oval head with pique′ drapes. One of a pair, which in itself is a rarity for this kind of hatpin. (Collection: Author's)

84

85

**PLATE 12**

(Collection: Doris Gaston, unless otherwise noted.)

**Left (Bottom to Top)**     **Description**

HATPIN HOLDER with 3 hatpins: 5½ ″ overall on 2¼ ″ base. Molded plastic in distinct Art Deco geometric design. Unusual and rare turquoise color plastic. Circa 1920. This type of hatpin holder is usually found in "French Ivory" color, which imitates the natural ivory elephant tusk. (Collection:                                                Author's)

HATPINS in above hatpin holder: Many Egyptian designs were again popularized during the Art Deco period. The discovery of the Valley of the King's burial site, followed by the opening of Tut's tomb, reintroduced the great fascination for anything Egyptian. These motifs were made of molded plastics during the height of the Art Deco craze. Three such examples are shown here, including a rare combination plastic and brass. The Pharoh in molded and painted plastic, and a symbolic scarab in gilded brass. (Collection: Author's)

Top, (Left to Right)

1.      Hatpin, 3¼ ″ long, including brass goblet-type finding, joined to a 4 5/16 ″ tempered steel pin. A ¾ ″ disc, tops the accordian pleated celluloid Art Deco ornament. Circa 1920. (Collection: Author's)

2.      Hatpin, 2 ″ x 2 ″ molded plastic head with 1/8 ″ tubular finding mounted on 4½ ″ steel pin. Papyrus leaf, Egyptian motif in geometric pattern typical of the Art Deco period. Circa 1922.

3.      Hatpin, 2¼ ″ x 2½ ″ overall plastic, double mold, ram's horn. Tubular finding joins 4 ″ pin to the Art Deco ornament. Circa 1920.

Bottom, (Left to Right)

1.      Hatpin, 3¼ ″ molded plastic feather and flame design, incorporating tiny molded plastic bugle bead forms. These have been painted to resemble real beads. A 1/16 ″ brass tubular finding connects this unique Art Deco ornament to a 4½ ″ brass pin. Hatpin is reminiscent of Victorian era beaded parlorwork. Circa 1925.

2.      Hatpin, 1¼ ″ round, molded ceramic porcelain painted head, bezel mounted in a brass button-type sleeve, joined to an 8½ ″ steel pin with a 1/16 ″ tubular finding. Eye of Horis motif, popularized in Art Deco era. Circa 1920. (Collection: Author's)

3.      Hatpin, 1½ ″ x 2½ ″ free form design in a two-mold mottled color plastic on a 7 ″ steel pin. Art Deco period, circa 1925.

4.      Hatpin, 2 ″ overall, two-mold plastic circlet joined by a 1/16 ″ brass tubular finding, crimped to a 4¾ ″ brass pin. Circa 1925.

**PLATE 13**
(Collection: Author's, unless otherwise noted.)

**Row & No.**                            **Description**

Top, left        5 3/8" high x 2 1/8" square, with 12 pin holes. Green jasperware, exported from the Volkstedt-Rudolstadt area in the Thuringian forest. Many porcelain factories there still produce porcelain and pottery for export. It is the equivalent of the Staffordshire area, England, in which are located various companies producing pottery and porcelain. (Example: center haptin holder, from Royal Doulton.) The crown and sunburst, with letter "R" incised, as in this jasperware hatpin holder, has been attributed to Schaffer & Vater (S&V mark), a company located in the Volkstedt-Rudolstadt area from 1890 to 1918. This company reportedly burned into ruin in 1918, but many of the most desirable and unique bisque hatpin holders bear the crown and sunburst incised mark. (Collection: Milly Combs)

Top, center   4¾" high, handpainted hunt scene (man on horseback). Marked: ROYAL DOULTON. Impressed trademark, circa 1902-1922: "Lambeth and Burslem Co., England". (Collection: Mrs. G.W. McCurdy)

Top, right    5½" high, solid base pearlized and beaded bisque art nouveau, iridescent enamelling and applied glass beading. Unglazed portrait. Base incised with crown and sunburst, letter "R". Attributed to Schaffer & Vater (S&V mark), located in the Volkstedt-Rudolstadt area of Germany, where there is a natural abundance of fuel and clay for pottery and porcelain. Circa 1905.

Row 2, 1.    3½" high, 2 1/8" solid base, marked with trademark of Goss China Company, England. Imprinted: W.H. Goss. This is the only souvenir hatpin holder made by this company, which prides itself on souvenir crest china pieces. The crest on this hatpin holder is "City of York". Goss china is often mistaken for Beleek.

Row 2, 2.    4¾" high solid-base. Equisitely hand-painted art nouveau motif, with heavy gold overlay on top. Painting initialed by artist: "HR". Base marked, "Hand-painted China, W.A. Pickard -- N & Co. -- France".

Row 3, 1.    4" high, marked "Japan", with artist's signature in Oriental caligraphy. Rare blue and white export china, with Occidental Dutch windmill scene. Rare.

Row 3, 2.    4¾" high x 2¾", porcelain, handpainted with heavy gold overlay. Eight-footed, with art nouveau floral in the mold. Nineteen pinholes. Marked: "Vienna Austria", and signed, "O'Haver". (Collection: Milly Combs)

Row 3, 3.    4½" high, unmarked souvenir, solid base. Pearlized porcelain with commemorative ceramic transfer portrait: "H M King George V". Circa 1910. With the death of Edward VII, the "Edwardian Period" of opulance began to decline, as did the innovative art nouveau influence. [Edward VII, eldest son of Queen Victoria, was king for less than a decade, 1901-1910.] This historical hatpin holder is a highly collectible commemorative.

Row 4, 1.    4¾" high, solid base. Handpainted in high art nouveau flourish w/heavy gold overlay. Trademarked, "hand-painted china, W.A. Pickard-Rosenthal-Gebrauchemusterschutz". Rosenthal/Pickard names reflect higher prices in all porcelain objects.

Row 4, 2.    4¾" high, solid base. Silver overlay on fine Bavarian china. Heavy silver overlay on top, which has 10 pin-holes. Note similarity in mold to hatpin on left. Green mark: Z.S.&Co., BAVARIA. Artist's initials in silver: EBC.

Row 4, 3.    5½" high souvenir holder, solid base marked, "Willow Art China, Longton". Handpainted words: HAT PIN, and ceramic transfer design inscribed "Jerusalem". English.

Row 4, 4.    5 1/8" x 2¾" base, SNE, Nagoya, Nippon green mark. Fine moriage work, gold beading. (Collection: Milly Combs)

## PLATE 14
(Collection: Dena Archer)
## VANITY OR TOILETTE SET

It was not unusual for women interested in china painting, to select particular white china blanks from various companies, and paint them as a matching set. This vanity or toilette set, is an excellent example of this, and shows some of the many pieces of varied shapes utilized in this fashion. All are handpainted.

Pin tray with finger-loop handle - 4″ x 5½″, unmarked.

Ring tree with interesting applied configuration to accomodate several rings. 5½″ x 3¾″, w/2″ tall ring tree. This piece is marked PL LIMOGES, FRANCE, and signed by the painter, "Mueller". Circa 1905.

Cologne bottle with stopper - incised letter G. 3¾″ bottle with a 2¼″ stopper.

Talc shaker - 4¼″ x 2¾″, with 19 holes. Solid bottom with cork-sized hole. Unmarked, but signed by painter, "Mueller".

Powder box with lid - unmarked. 4¾″ dish, 5″ top, with a 1″ finial.

Hatpin Holder - unmarked. 5″ tall with 3″ saucer, and 16 pin-holes.

Tray - unusually large 13″ x 16″, marked LIMOGES, FRANCE, W.G. & CO. (bracketed). Handpainted and signed, "Mueller". Mark is William Guerin Company, exporter of white ware, 1891-1915, when it then merged and expanded with other Limoges porcelain factories.

## PLATE 15
(Collection: Dena Archer)
VANITY SET (Top)

Tray - 8¼ ″ x 11¼ ″, marked: LIMOGES, FRANCE (W.G. & Co.), handpainted. Mark is of the William Guerin Company, that exported much white ware and used this mark after 1891, up to approximately 1915 when it expanded and consolidated with other porcelain companies.

Hatpin Holder - marked VIENNA AUSTRIA, (Crown w/2 shields). 5″ high, 1¾ ″ base, w/16 pin-holes.

Ring tree - (shown bottom, left) marked BAVARIA. 3½ ″ saucer, 2-5/8″ tall, heavily overlaid with gold.

Powder box - (covered), marked VIENNA AUSTRIA (in a Crown). 4¼ ″ round, w/top lid.

Trinket box - (oblong shape), marked FRANCE GDA (incised numeral 6). 2¼ ″ x 4¼ ″ w/lid.

HATPIN HOLDER with covered trinket box (attached)
(bottom, right)
Fitted and notched lid. Mark: Eagle, fish & star (green mark). Handpainted ovelay, heavy gold accents. Ceramic transfer with overpainted highlights. 2½ ″ x 4″ lid for attached box which has a 1″ depth. Holder measures 4½ ″ high w/14 pin-holes. Rare.

## PLATE 16

(Collection: Author's, unless otherwise noted.)

**Row & No.**              **Description**

Top        8″ steel pin, 1½″ handpainted ceramic head, in button-sleeve brass mounting, bezel-set. Colors and design in Art Deco fashion. Circa 1913. Rare.

Row 2, 1. 7¾″ steel pin, 2″ head depicting lilies of the valley. Reverse marked: "Genuine Cloisonne, Sterling". Vermeil, [gilt over silver]. Hallmarked: Crown, passant lion, and letter "W", signifying Sheffield, England, 1914. Lily of the Valley is the flower for the month of May. There was a "hatpin of the month", in this series, as will be noted in the next hatpin, showing December's poinsettia.

Row 2, 2. Same as No. 1, excpet that flower is December's poinsettia. Exquisitely rendered series.

Row 2, 3. Although same measurements as No. 1, and No. 2, this Lotus blossom, or water lily, is hallmarked London, 1907. Fine basse-taille enameling, and marked on reverse: "genuine cloisonne". (Collection: Milly Combs)

Row 3, 1. 9″ steel pin, with a 1½″ round x 1″ depth, narrowing to fit into a 3/16″ cup finding. Fine ceramic porcelain portrait, embellished with heavy gold overlay and beading. Overpainting accents the ceramic transfer. Rare.

Row 3, 2 12″ steel pin, 1¼″ head, Japanese cloisonne, with foil back. Button-sleeve metallic mounting. Marked in Japanese letters. Rare type of cloisonne hatpin. (Collection: Milly Combs)

Row 3, 3. 7¼″ steel pin, 1¼″ diameter ceramic transfer portrait, with cobalt blue porcelain mounting set into a small metallic sleeve then attached to pin. Embellished with gold. Attributed to Limoge factory porcelain. (Collection: Dena Archer)

Bottom    11″ steel pin, 1½″ round basse-taille enamelled head, over-painted with roses. Gold trim. (Collection: Dena Archer)

**Plate No.**                     **Description**
17        Vanity Hatpin, 1½ " round, measuring 2 " from bottom of art nouveau brass mounting to top of large faceted red bezel-set stone. Star-shaped decoration atop lid, features 32 prong-set rhinestones in foiled cups. Convex mirror fits into lid; a lamb's wool powder puff housed in bottom. 11½ " steel pin. (Collection: Doris Gaston)(Photo Credit: Dave Hammell)

Plate No.    Description
18A    Hatpin Holder. Royal
Bayreuth (Blue Mark),
"Clover" figural. 4½"
high, 2¼" solid bottom.
13 pin-holes. (Collection:
Robert V. Larsen)(Photo
Credit: Jim Frieze Studio,
Columbus, Nebraska)

Plate No.    Description
18B    Hatpin Holder. Royal
Bayreuth (Blue Mark)
"Art Nouveau Lady"
figural. 4½" high w/3½"
saucer base. Solid bot-
tom. 16 pin-holes. Rare.
(Collection: Robert V.
Larsen)(Photo Credit: Jim
Frieze Studio, Columbus,
Nebraska)

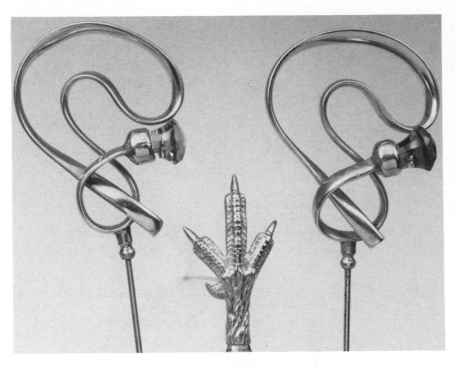

**Plate No.**                     **Description**

19       Pair Charles Horner design adapted by Histler, unmarked, one with topaz color and one with amythest color thistle-cut stones. 9¾ " steel pins, with 1½ " x 2 " overall ornament. Thistle-cut sets each measure 3/16 ". Silver plate. Circa 1910. (Collection: Doris Gaston)(Photo Credit: Dave Hammell)

Center hatpin: ¾ " Falcon's claw, set with cairgorm. Typical Scottish design. 9½ " steel pin. Unmarked. Finely etched and engraved. (Collection: Doris Gaston)(Photo Credit: Dave Hammell)

**Plate No.** **Description**
20A     Hatpin Holder. Royal Bayreuth (Blue Mark) "Crocus" figural. 4¾" high, 1¾" solid base. 16 pin-holes. (Collection: Robert V. Larsen)(Photo Credit: Jim Frieze)

**Plate No.** **Description**
20B     Hatpin Holder. Royal Bayreuth (Blue Mark) Sunbonnet Baby series, "Washing". 4¾" tall, 4" saucer, solid base. Rare. (Collection: Robert V. Larsen)(Photo Credit: Jim Frieze Studio, Columbus, Ohio)

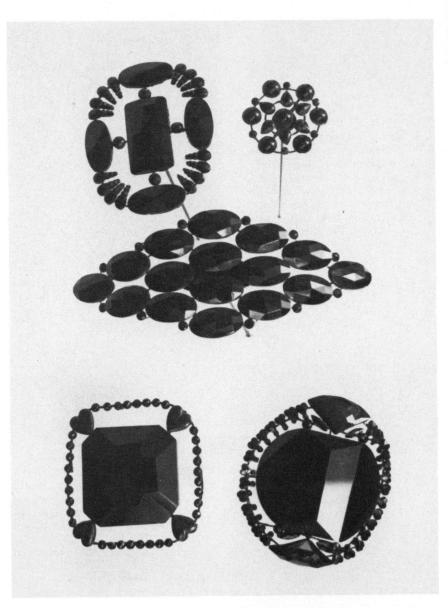

Plate No.                    Description
21            Five variations of rivited jet glass hatpins, shown reduced half-size.
              Each cut and faceted stone is individually soldered to a wire frame.
              Pin-shanks are japanned steel. Hatpins are from Her Majesty's sup-
              plier, Gebruder Feix, Albrechtsdorf, Jablonecer District, Czech. Circa
              1875. (Collection: Author's)(Photo Credit: Ed Wetzork)

| Plate No. | Description |
|---|---|
| 22 | Vanity Hatpins. |

Vanity Hatpins. In this category, are compacts, rouge-rag depositories, perfume holders and scented plush lids, as well as a storage receptacle for "emergency" straight pins (shown here). Both examples are 1¾" gilt over brass, in varied art nouveau frames. Simulated jade, turquoise, amythest, and topaz, in cabachon-cut bezel-set stones, were beautiful accents to the hinged and clasped lids. 8" brass pin-shanks are attached to ornament with brass findings. Circa 1913. (Collection: Doris Gaston)(Photo Credit: Dave Hammell)

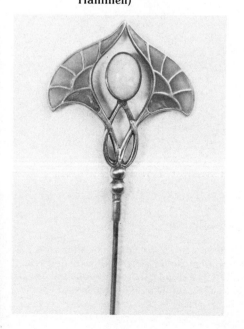

Plate No.    Description
23    Plique'-a-jour hatpin. 1¼" x 1½" head on 7½" silver pin. Reverse side of ornament marked: Depose' with numerals 900 in circle. Small punch-mark. Exquisite green-yellow-blue transparent enamelling. Art nouveau design accented with bezel-set genuine opal. (Collection: Shirley Babcock)(Photo Credit: Ponds Studio, San Marcos, Texas)

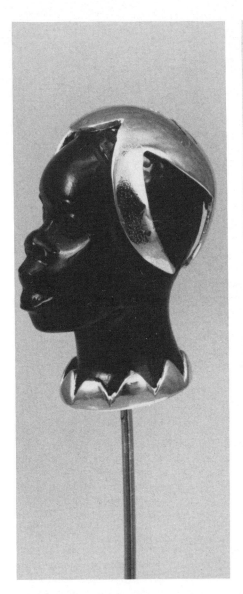

**Plate No.**                   **Description**
**24A &**
**24B**      Figural hatpin, 1¼ " Moor's head, with ½ " scalloped collar atop 7 " rolled gold pin-shank. Heavy Roman Gold helmet with crest and scorpion. Unknown artist's punchmark. Hand carved and polished onyx. One-of-a-kind hatpin. Rare. (Collection: Doris Gaston)(Photo Credit: Dave Hammell)

## Plate No. 25
### Description
Hatpin, figural American eagle. Silver, 1¾" x 1¼". Prong-set, faceted ruby-color stone accent for eye. Thirty-one pave' set rhinestones enrich the etched and beautifully engraved high repousse' work. 7½" steel pin, including silver finding. Rare. Circa 1876, possibly a memento of America's Centennial. (Collection: Doris Gaston)(Photo Credit: Dave Hammell)

| Plate No. | Description |
|---|---|
| 26 | Three views of a rare, patented hatpin. (Left) 1½" ornamental head, gilt over brass, with ¾" bezel-set amythest color faceted stone, shown tilted in a position whereby the small hook above the pin-shank can readily attach to a fabric. The fabric was usually the hat-band of a woman's hat, which had been removed from the wearer and safely stored alongside a dining table, or the 12" steel pin-shank could be plunged into the plush backing of a theatre seat. "LADIES, PLEASE REMOVE YOUR HATS", was a notice flashed on a movie-screen, or placed in view on a standard alongside a theatre curtain. The advertisement for this unique hatpin, promotes the benefits of ownership: "NO MORE MASHED MILLINERY". The necessity of removing the enormous concoctions of feathers, flowers, and be-ribboned chapeau during theatre presentations or during dining-hall stage-shows, is obvious. (Center) The machine-stamped brass head is gilded and the fine glass center stone required no foil backing. (Right) Note the ¼" hook at lower right. When the ornamental head is upright, this hook is safely tucked under the cleverly contrived mounting for the ornament. Tubular brass finding joins pin-shank to head. Circa 1905. (Collection: Doris Gaston)(Photo Credit: Dave Hammell) |

**Plate No.**                                    **Description**

27        Hatpin Holder. "Strawberries on a Brick Tower". Crown & Sunburst "R" (S&V Mark). 5″ tall x 2½″ x 2½″ wide. Solid base with 12 pinholes. (See color plate #13, top row number 1.)(Collection: Audrae Heath)(Photo Credit: Tom Heath)

Plate No.                  **Description**
28       Wall hanging hatpin holder. Crown & Sunburst "R" (S&V Mark),
6¾" long, bisque, with 6 pinholes in a fancy reticulated top. White
cameo, teal background in gold wreath.

        Bell shaped stickpin holder, marked same as above. 2¼" tall
with solid bottom and 12 pinholes. Green/gray bisque with white
cameo and trim, suggestive of authentic Wedgwood decoration. Rare.
Circa 1905. (Collection: Audrae Heath)(Photo Credit: Tom Heath)

**Plate No.**              **Description**
29        Chocolate Glass hatpin holder. Rare. 7 7/8″ tall, 2 5/8″ diameter.
Attributed to Indiana-Greentown or Fenton Glass by Rosenthal. Circa
1905. (Collection: Audrae Heath)(Photo Credit: Tom Heath)

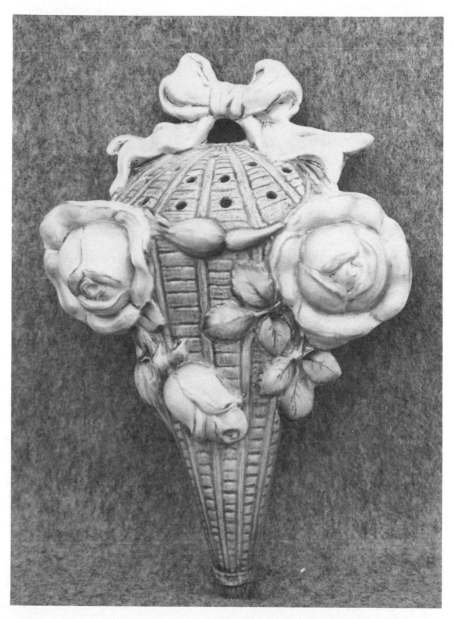

| Plate No. | Description |
| --- | --- |
| 30 | Wall type hatpin holder. Hanging basket with roses. Crown & Sunburst "R" (S&V Mark). 6½" long x 4" wide with 11 pinholes. Painted in matte finish pastels. Pale beige basketweave, blue ribbon. Rare. Circa 1910. (Collection: Audrae Heath)(Photo Credit: Tom Heath) |

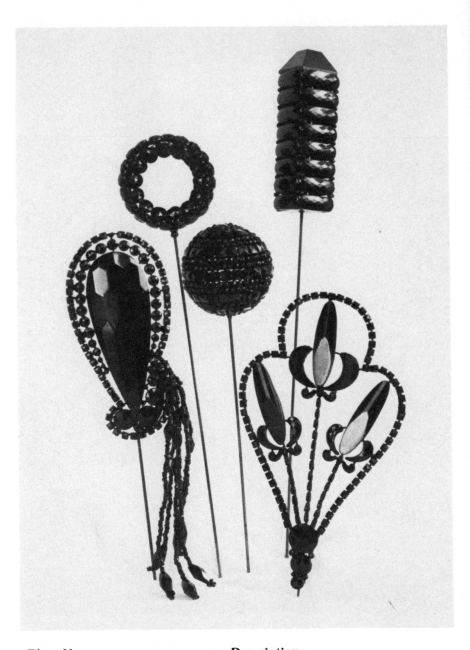

**Plate No.**
31

**Description**

Assortment of elegant rivited jet glass hatpins with japanned pin-shanks. (See Plate 21 for complete description of this highly collectible type of hatpin.)(Collection: Author's)(Photo Credit: Ed Wetzork)

**Plate No.**                  **Description**
32         Hatpin Holder. Royal Doulton English porcelain. 5″ tall x 3½″ diameter. Solid base, with 7 pinholes. Lovely miniature painting of Shakespeare's "Ophelia". Lavender and pinks on dark creme background. Dark green trim. Rare. (Collection: Audrae Heath)(Photo Credit: Tom Heath)

**Plate No.** **Description**
33 Figural hatpin holder. Bear and a brick tower. Very rare Crown & Sunburst "R" (S&V Mark). 4¼" tall x 3½" wide, with 13 pinholes. Solid base. Bear painted brown or black, on ivory-painted tower. (Collection: Audrae Heath)(Photo Credit: Tom Heath)

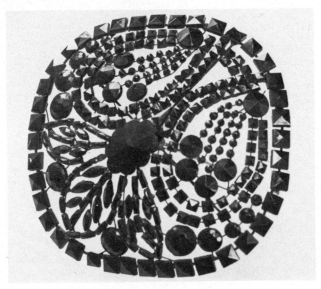

**Plate No.** **Description**
34 Hatpin showing variations of cut and faceted jet glass stones rivited to a wire frame. Frame measures 3¼", with ¼" japanned funnel-shaped finding and 1/8" bulbous finding crimped to a 12" japanned pin-shank. (See Plate 21 for full description) Very rare and collectible hatpin. (Collection: Author's)(Photo Credit: Ed Wetzork)

110

**Plate No.**                             **Description**
35         Very rare art nouveau white porcelain hatpin holder. 3 5/8″ tall, solid bottom with 7 pin holes. Marked: L P Limoges. Necklace, set with large red stone, is identical to stone adorning center of model's forehead. Four pearl combs and flowers worn in hair. Colors of garment are soft pink-beiges. Peacock is painted in shades of delicate blues, greys and greens. Tiny gold beading decorates trim of gold overlay. Texture of filmy shawl gives the ceramic decal a handpainted appearance. Exquisite! (Collection: Audrae Heath)(Photo Credit: Tom Heath)

**Plate No.      Description**
36A      Royal Bayreuth (Blue Mark), "Corinthian" or "Classic" hatpin holder. 4¾" tall, 4" saucer base. Solid bottom with 16 pinholes. (Collection: Robert V. Larsen)(Photo Credit: Jim Frieze Studio, Columbus, Nebraska)

**Plate No.      Description**
36B      Royal Bayreuth (Blue Mark), "Portrait" Tapestry hatpin holder. 4½" tall, 2" reticulated, decorated solid base. 15 pinholes. Highly collectible. (Collection: Robert V. Larsen)(Photo Credit: Jim Frieze Studio, Columbus, Nebraska)

| Plate No. | Description |
|---|---|
| 37A & | |
| 37B | "The Eternal Question". Hatpin copied from the Gibson Girl illustration by Charles Dana Gibson. Posed by Evelyn Nesbit, (See 37B) also known as the "Girl in the Red Velvet Swing". Gilt over copper head, measuring 2″ long on 8″ steel pin. Rare. Circa 1890. Gibson's wife, the beautiful and fashionable Irene Langhorne, was the artist's model who set the style for every other "Gay Nineties" lady of fashion. (Unmarked) [Drawing from Heath collection](Collection: Audrae Heath)(Photo Credit: Tom Heath) |

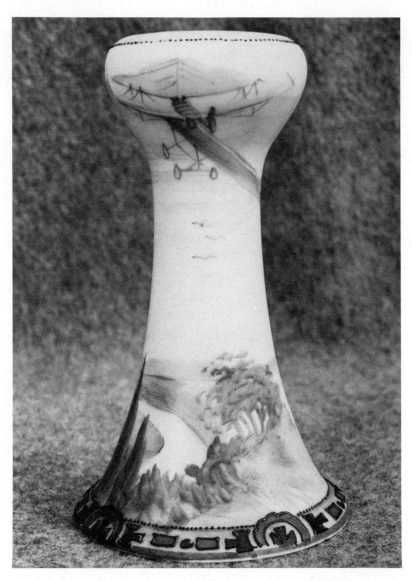

| Plate No. | Description |
| --- | --- |

38      Nippon Bleriot Airplane series. Hatpin holder is rare. 4¾ " tall, solid bottom, open-top. The Bleriot designed plane (1907-1909) crossed the English Channel, July 25, 1909 from Calais to Dover in 30 minutes. Louis Bleriot was the first to accomplish this feat. Souvenir holder is handpainted in lavender, green, and rust colors with trims accented with beading and moriage work. (Collection: Audrae Heath)(Photo Credit: Tom Heath)

**Plate No.**                      **Description**
39       Enlarged to show detail of hand-cut crystal hatpin head with a blown teardrop-shape inside. Note bezel-type patch finding that attaches the 2½ ″ heavy colorless quartz ornament (crystal), to the 10½ ″ brass pin. Rare. (Collection: Audrae Heath)(Photo Credit: Tom Heath)

115

**Plate No.**                               **Description**

40        Scarab (beetle), 1½″ x 1¼″ figural hatpin, German silver. Green enamelled wings and body and red enamelled eyes. 10″ pin-shank. (Collection: Audrae Heath)(Photo Credit: Tom Heath)

| Plate No. | Description |
|---|---|
| 41 | Portrait hatpins are highly collectible, and this sterling silver is a fine example. Marked: "silver front". 7/8″ head on 7½″ pin. Possibly Gorham or Unger Bros. (American) (Collection: Audrae Heath)(Photo Credit: Tom Heath) |

117

**Plate No.**                    **Description**

42        Double mold, back-to-back, art nouveau sterling silver head. Note detail of etched and engraved feathers and flowers in headdress. High repousse' in face and configuration of hair that entwines a patch-type finding which attaches to 1¼ " head. 7½ " pin. Hollow ornament. (Collection: Audrae Heath)(Photo Credit: Tom Heath)

**Plate No.**                    **Description**
43          One of a series of punched out coins. 1908 Liberty Nickle, U.S.A.,
            Patented Nov. 22, 1904. Cross-bar on back of coin, with tubular fin-
            ding, anchors head to 9″ nickle pin-shanks. Some hatpins were
            mounted on 10″ & 12″ pin-shanks. Others in series includes: 1910
            & 1918 Liberty Dimes, 1917 Liberty half-dollar, 1908 Indian Head
            Penny, and foreign coins such as 1904 Republic of Panama. Lincoln
            copper pennies were favorites. (Collection: Audrae Heath)(Photo
            Credit: Tom Heath)

| Plate No. | Description |
| --- | --- |
| 44A | 5¼ " pink and white bisque w/solid bottom and 12 pin holes. Egyptian motif repeated each side. Manufactured in several colors, some have been hand painted rather crudely in bright blue, red, and yellow. Circa 1909. (Collection: Audrae Heath)(Photo Credit: Tom Heath) |

| Plate No. | Description |
| --- | --- |
| 44B | 5½ " Art Nouveau hatpin holder. Lavender bisque w/gold trim. Solid bottom, and 7 pin holes. Available in antique white, pink, and lavender, many have a pale green wash; other examples are found with applied enamelled beading in various colors and with high iridescent accents. (Collection: Audrae Heath)(Photo Credit: Tom Heath) |

| Plate No. | Description |
| --- | --- |
| 44C | 5½ " Art Nouveau beautifully detailed mold. Solid bottom and 7 pin holes. Made in several soft pastel shades complementary to bisquewares. Some have hand painted gold accents and trim. (Collection: Audrae Heath)(Photo Credit: Tom Heath) |

| Plate No. | Description |
| --- | --- |
| 44D | 4¾ " figural Geisha Girl, available in lavender or pink bisque, with pale green wash accented the crevices of kimono, fan, and other folds. Solid bottom w/seven pin holes trimmed in gold. This hatpin holder is more rare in high glaze firing of antique white, rather than unglazed bisque. |

A

B

C

D

The hatpin holders shown this page are all incised with the S&V mark of Schaffer & Vater, (1890-1918), Voldstedt-Rudolstadt area. This mark is the Crown and Sunburst with letter "R" incised in bisque. Other numerals incised with the mark are factory identification of mold. All hatpin holders from the Audrae Heath collection, photographed by Tom Heath.

121

| Plate No. | Description |
| --- | --- |
| 45A | 5¼" green and white jasperware. Varied figures of antiquity influence design. Solid bottom and 7 pin holes. (Collection: Audrae Heath)(Photo Credit: Tom Heath) |

| Plate No. | Description |
| --- | --- |
| 45B | 4½" blue jasperware "Kewpie" hatpin holder. Incised S&V mark, plus "Rose O'Neill Kewpie, Germany", and manufacturer's identifying numbers. Solid bottom and 8 pin holes. Highly collectible. [The most rare is the same holder in smaller 4" mold-size] (Collection: Audrae Heath)(Photo Credit: Tom Heath) |

| Plate No. | Description |
| --- | --- |
| 45C | 5" pink bisque with pale blue trim. Dark blue frames cameos which are different profiles either side. Solid bottom and seven pin holes. (Collection: Audrae Heath)(Photo Credit: Tom Heath) |

| Plate No. | Description |
| --- | --- |
| 45D | 4½" triangular shape, antique white bisque with handpainted pastel wash over raised figures in pastoral scene. Scroll work highlighted with gold. Solid bottom and ten pin holes. (Collection: Audrae Heath)(Photo Credit: Tom Heath) |

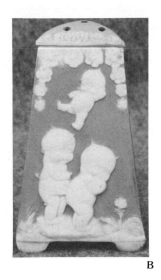

B

A

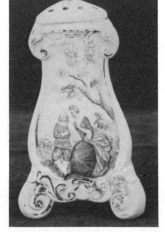

C

D

Hatpin holders shown this page are all incised with the S&V mark of Schaffer & Vater, (1890-1918), Voldstedt-Rudolstadt area. This mark is the Crown and Sunburst with letter "R" incised in bisque. Other numerals incised with the mark are factory identification of mold. All hatpin holders from the Audrae Heath collection, photographed by Tom Heath.

123

| Plate No. | Description |
|---|---|
| 46A | 5¼" combination stickpin and hatpin holder w/solid base. Variant cameos each side in dark green on antique white; pale green & pink trim. Four holes in festooned urn, plus seven in hatpin holder. Dark red berries in greenery. (Collection: Audrae Heath)(Photo Credit: Tom Heath) |

| Plate No. | Description |
|---|---|
| 46B | 5" bisque holder with identical rust-colored cameos either side. Solid base. Antique white, pale green & pink trim; two Rams' heads support dark red berries in greenery. Manufactured in several color combinations, bright blue being rarest. (Collection: Audrae Heath)(Photo Credit: Tom Heath) |

| Plate No. | Description |
|---|---|
| 46C | 4½" pink & white bisque w/olive green cameo. (Different cameos each side) Solid base. Seven pin holes. Made in several pastel colors. (Collection: Audrae Heath)(Photo Credit: Tom Heath) |

| Plate No. | Description |
|---|---|
| 46D | 5½" antique white bisque, w/pale green and pink trim. Identical olive green cameos each side. Seven pin holes outlined in gold with raised pink-painted flowers. (Collection: Audrae Heath)(Photo Credit: Tom Heath) |

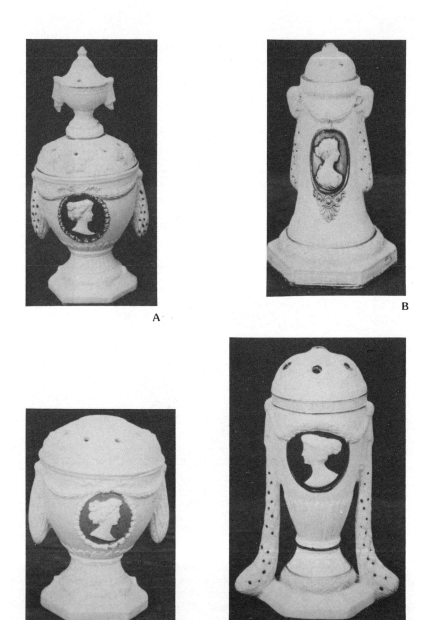

A

B

C

D

The four hatpin holders shown this page are all incised with the S&V mark of Schaffer & Vater, (1890-1918). This Crown and Sunburst with "R" incised in bisqueware, has various numbers identifying the design of that particular mold. All hatpins holders shown are from the Audrae Heath collection, photographed by Tom Heath.

**Plate 47**

## AUTHENTIC TYPE JEWELRY FINDINGS USED FOR
## ATTACHING THE HATPIN ORNAMENT TO PIN

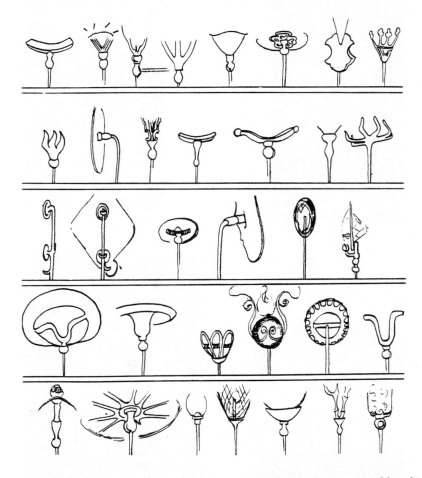

Study the above drawings carefully and note how the ornamental head is attached to the pin-shank by use of various jewelers' "Findings":

Inverted arc or bridge type; tubular shapes, crimped to pin-shank; fancy patch-types; pronged; flanged; cupped; Tiffany-type mounting with delicate prongs; funnel-shaped findings; cross-bar anchorage, etc. In every instance, except where the pin has been inserted into a drilled hole of a faceted stone, all hatpin heads are mounted to the pin-shank with particular care to cover the joining-section with a finding. This method not only makes for a more attractive hatpin, but serves to provide a secure, permanent, juncture.

FOR OTHER TYPE PIN-SHANKS,
see NOMENCLATURE for HATPINS

**Plate 48**

## PIN-SHANKS, PATCHES, VARIOUS MOUNTINGS AND JOINS FOR HATPINS

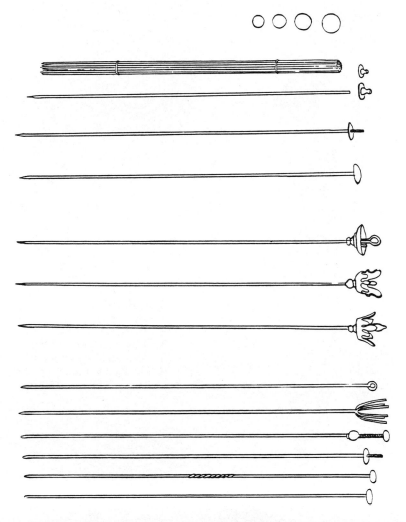

Look for the above type of mounting devices used in authentic hatpins.

These are the "working parts" of an ornamental hatpin. They were manufactured to serve the jeweler's needs, and were made by pin manufacturers and producers of jewelry findings to the trade.

Study the drawings carefully. Familiarize yourself with the types of pins and findings utilized in authentic Period Hatpins.

FOR OTHER TYPE PIN-SHANKS
see NOMENCLATURE for HATPINS

Plate 49

See GLOSSARY
1 & 2 - "Nibs".
3 - Escutcheon type hatpin.
4 - Engraved top of escutcheon.
5 - "Nodder" type hatpin.
6 - A "figural mounting" type.
7 - A "*Full* Figural" hatpin.

For further types of specialized
pin-shanks, see NOMENCLATURE FOR HATPINS.

**Plate 50**

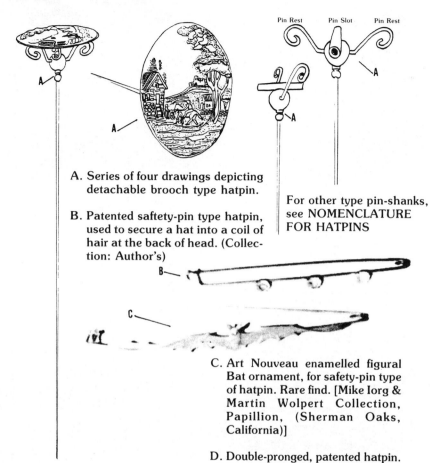

A. Series of four drawings depicting detachable brooch type hatpin.

B. Patented saftety-pin type hatpin, used to secure a hat into a coil of hair at the back of head. (Collection: Author's)

For other type pin-shanks, see NOMENCLATURE FOR HATPINS

C. Art Nouveau enamelled figural Bat ornament, for safety-pin type of hatpin. Rare find. [Mike Iorg & Martin Wolpert Collection, Papillion, (Sherman Oaks, California)]

D. Double-pronged, patented hatpin. [From original specifications, courtesy Mrs. Dennis C. Horton]

A.D. 1912 July 3 No. 15,522
HISKINS & others' Complete Sepcification

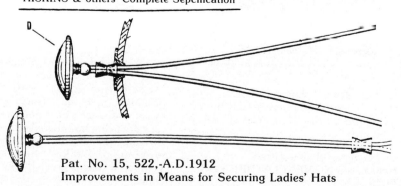

Pat. No. 15, 522,-A.D.1912
Improvements in Means for Securing Ladies' Hats

129

**Plate 51**

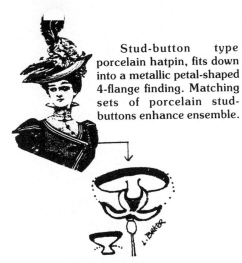

Stud-button type porcelain hatpin, fits down into a metallic petal-shaped 4-flange finding. Matching sets of porcelain stud-buttons enhance ensemble.

A full card of "point protectors", and illustration of how they were used. [Photo: Carol King. From the Carol King Collection.]

For further types of specialized pin-shanks, see NOMENCLATURE FOR HATPINS.

A paper packaged tempered steel common hatpins, of the "shoe-button glass" variety. Available in black, white, and (rare) sky-blue. The small glass tops are being hammered off, and the pin-shanks utilized in the making of "fake" hatpins. Tempered steel is greyish-blue in color.

Plate 52

## Reproductions and Fakes
## STUDY THE SHAPES CAREFULLY

(Top, L-R) "Flow Blue" reproduction holders, "Moss Rose" & "Romantic" patterns, (English); German mold reproduced in Japan; woman's bust, both sides, in *new* mold (Japan).

(Center, L-R) Repro of German mold originally made for Sears, Roebuck (c.1910), now made in Japan; three unmarked reproductions (Japan).

(Bottom, L-R) Copies of R.S. Prussia molds and "Flow Blue" holder and ring tree reproduction (England). Many reproductions have newly applied ceramic decals. (See P. 132)

(Photo, Left) An *authentic* hatpin holder, R.S. Prussia, (red mark). This fine *old* piece has *newly applied* ceramic transfer of portrait. "Pinkie", "Blue Boy", animals, etc. falsely raises price.

# Plate 53

Decal Size →

Enlargement of R.S. Prussia Mark.

A. R.S. PRUSSIA reproduced ceramic decal. Hatpin Holders and stickpin holders are being reproduced & this decal appears on base. It is not under the glaze.

B. A newly designed combination hatpin holder & ring tree. China blanks are imported from Japan and are being handpainted then sold at shops and shows.

C. Reproduced cut and engraved cut glass hatpin holders, available in blue, red, or clear glass.

D. G.W. Huntley Company catalogue, showing American cut glass hatpin holders circa 1905.

HATPIN HOLDER
Panama pattern
Height 8¼ inches
No. K35334 . . $8.75

HATPIN HOLDER
Bremen patern
Height 8¼ inches
No. K35335 . $11.25

**Plate 54**

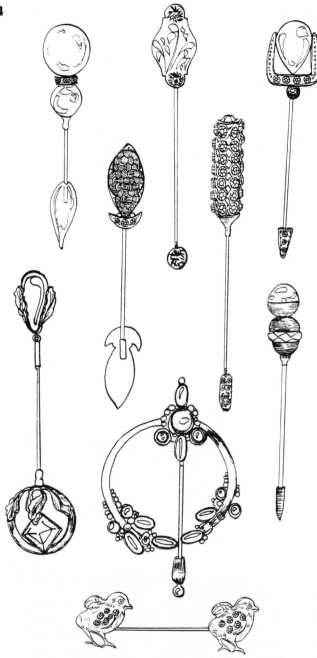

**AN ASSORTMENT OF HAT ORNAMENTS
WITH VARIOUS SHAPED NIBS**

# SECTION III.

## CHAPTER I
## GLOSSARY

## CHAPTER II
## HATPIN NOMENCLATURE

# CHAPTER I
## GLOSSARY
### (Including specific hatpin-related terminology)

*For complementary GLOSSARIES published by COLLECTOR BOOKS, that are related to this handbook, refer to the author's titles: "100 Years of Collectible Jewelry, (1850-1950)", and "Art Nouveau & Art Deco Jewelry". Both publications also contain many fine hatpins in full color.*

ACCENTS
> To accentuate an ornamental hatpin head with small brilliants, metallic design, natural elements, rattles or bells -- anything added to the overall design or mounting which enhances the ornament.

ART DECO
> 1910-1925 era of stilted, stylized design, influenced by the American Indian, ancient Egyptian art, Greek and Roman architecture -- but mainly refers to the transition from Art Nouveau's free-flowing fanciful curvilear lines to the graphic geometric line; from the lackadaisical to speed motifs.

ART NOUVEAU
> Introduced in the late 19th Century - 1892-1910, it was a short-lived period of design which introduced undulating curves, spirals, and flowing lines. It followed hard upon the classical and "romantic" Aesthetic period, being greatly influenced by it and the "pure, back to nature" Arts and Crafts Movement championed by William Morris and his clique.

BAROQUE
> Bold, ornate, "heavy looking", elaborate frames and mountings for hatpins.

BEAD
> A round or free-form object, usually of glass, wood, ivory, coral, etc., with a hole end-to-end, through the material. When used singly as a hatpin head, the bead is inserted on to the pin-shank, and a jeweler's finding "stops" the bead from slipping off the top, while another prevents it from sliding down the pin-shank.

BEZEL SETTING
> A manner of mounting a stone in which a groove or flange holds the stone securely in its setting.

BOX SETTING
> A stone enclosed in a "box" with the edges of the metal pressed down to hold it in place.

BRASS
> A yellowish-gold color which is primarily an alloy of copper, tin, and zinc, or other base metals. The majority of manufactured hatpins were in brass.

CAMEO
> Cut, carved, or engraved conch shell, onyx gemstone, or coral, carved or exploited so that the various colored layers contrast the design in relief. Cameos of molded glass or synthetics seek to imitate the natural element

of shell, gemstone or coral; some molded glass cameos are portraits without variation in color, relying on the high-low relief of pattern to achieve effect.

## CARAT or KARAT

CARAT - term for unit weight of gemstones, but particularly of precious gems such as diamonds, i.e, 1 ct. diamond. GOLD KARAT SHOULD BE PROFESSIONALLY APPRAISED SINCE GENUINE GEMS-/GEMSTONES ARE USUALLY INVOLVED IN THE GOLD MOUNTING. KARAT - term for measure of gold tabled at 1/24th part of pure gold in an alloy, i.e., 14K, 18K, or 24K.

## CARNIVAL GLASS

Specifically iridescent glass made in America from 1910-1930. Usually in pressed patterns, it was mostly manufactured by Northwood Glass, Co., Ohio; Imperial Glass Company, Ohio; and The Fenton Art Glass Company, West Virginia.

## CARTOUCHE'

A shield or scroll with curved edges used particularly on silver for a monogram. A cartouche' is NOT AN ESCUTCHEON. An escutcheon is a plate of metal added or applied to the top of a signet-type or monogram-type hatpin head.

## CERAMIC TRANSFER

A design engraved on a copper plate which is linked; then an impression is taken on a piece of tissue paper. This is transferred to a piece of porcelain. The transfer is then hand-colored with tinting, then covered by a glaze and re-fired. Some ceramic transfers are already available in colored inks so as not to require over-painting to give the "handpainted" look to some porcelain pieces.

## CHANNEL SETTING

A series of stones set close together in a straight line, in which sides of mounting grip outer edges of stones.

## CHASING

A method of ornamenting metal with grooves and lines using an assortment of hand chisels and hammers. Flat chasing, (obverse side). If chasing is done from the back or reverse side, and raises the metal, it is called repousse'.

## CLAW SETTING

The use of tiny claws or prongs curved to hold down a gem or gemstone.

## CLOISONNE

Enameling in which thin wire is bent to form cells, (cloisons). These are then filled with enamel, each colour in a separate compartment. (See ENAMEL).

## CORAL (genuine)

Skeleton of the coral polyp which was highly popular in fashionable English Victorian circles. Most coral used in Victorian jewelry came from the Mediterranean.

## DAMASCENE
To inlay gold and silver into iron or steel in a decorative pattern, characteristic of ornaments from Damascus.

## DIE-STAMPING
A commercial, machine-made process which superceded hand-wrought and custom-made pieces of jewelry, including hatpins.

## DRAGON'S BREATH
A glass very popular 1910-1930, made to imitate the Mexican Fire Opal gemstone.

## ENAMEL
Enameling is a firing of melted glass. The powdered glass mixture is composed of feldspar, quartz, soda, borax, calcium phosphates and kaolin. Metallic oxides produce the various desired colors. There is little transparent, clear, see-through, colorless enameling; "translucent" is a more definitive term. But the word "transparent" has been an accepted term for plique'-a-jour enameling which permits light to pass through as in stained glass. There are several types of enameling:

Basse-Taille (bass-a-tie) - Metal plate cut to various depths into which translucent enamel is poured, thus achieving a 3-dimensional effect. The depth of relief produces shadings from light to dark. The deeper the metal is cut, the darker the color; where shallow routing occurs, the shading is almost transparent. This routing is worked intalgio, the opposite of repousse.

Champleve (shamp le-va) - An enameling technique in which areas of metal are hand cut, etched, or routed and filled with enamel. Unlike cloisonne, the cells are cut rather than formed by wires. Champleve is most commonly applied to copper or bronze. The metals are gilded on exposed and visible surfaces. Guilloche' technique differs in that the designs are machine-turned and etched, and then enamelled. This is a much faster process and many boxed sets of hatpins with matching stud buttons and buckles are representative of this technique and were enamelled primarily on copper and silver.

Cloisonne (kloi zo-na) - Enameling in which thin wire of silver, gold, bronze, or copper, is bent to form cells, (cloisons) and then filled with enamel. Each color is in a separate compartment, each compartment separated by thin wire that has often been gilded.

Limoges enamel (le-mozh) - A colorful application of enamel that depicts a portrait or scene similar to that which is rendered on canvas.

Niello enameling (ni-el-o) - The lines or incisions of a design are contrasted with the color of the metal, i.e., gold, silver, etc., by applying in several layers, a mixture of sulphur, lead, silver and copper which appears black when filled into the engraved metallic work. A blackish enamel work.

Plique'-A-Jour (ple-ka-a-jer) - A translucent cloisonne in which there is no metal backing for the enamel work. During firing, a metal supportive base is used until firing ceases; then when the piece has cooled and the enamel has hardened, the finished product no longer requires the base, so this support is removed. A most skillful technique.

## ENGRAVED

Cutting lines into metal, either decorative or symbolic, as for crest, initials, or monogram or intricate design motifs.

## ESCUTCHEON

A small metal plate used atop an ornamental hatpin for monogram or signet.

## FIGURAL MOUNTING

A figural form used as a SETTING to enhance a stone or artifact on hatpin heads. Not to be confused with a FULL figural hatpin head.

## FILIGREE

To apply thread-like wire and decorate into a lacy network or design.

## FINDINGS

Small patches, sockets, bushings, and other tiny tubular, bugle or funnel shaped, metallic parts used to finish or attach a hatpin head ornament to the pin-shank.

## FRAME

A word coined to describe the metallic framework which comprises a hatpin HEAD, with or without stones. Also, the metal which "frames" a simple or fancy chased design, or the framework which supports a gem or gemstone (genuine or glass), which is used as a hatpin head.

## FULL FIGURAL

A hatpin head which has no mounting or frame, but is comprised instead of a figural beast, bird, fish, flower, human, insect, reptile (natural form or mythological or improvised). The figural is a complete hatpin head and does not rely on a frame or setting, but becomes the entire ornament unto itself. A figural is often accented with tiny brilliants, especially used for eyes.

## GILT

Method used after the invention of electro-gilding. Gilding (gilt) is a process of plating a die-stamped piece of base metal to give it a real or pseudo gold or silver color. Most often, and more abundant, are gold color hatpins that have been gilded, rather than silver-color gilding.

## GOLD ELECTROPLATE (See GILT)

## GOLDSTONE

Man-made brown glass with specs of copper infused within, made as an imitation of Aventurine.

## GYPSY SETTING

(Also known as Bezel-set) In a gypsy setting, the top of the stone is exposed just above the flange of metal which holds the stone securely in its mounting.

## HALLMARK

An official mark first adopted in England which is incised, punched, or stamped on gold or silver to show quality and to signify purity of metal according to "sterling" or "carat" standard. Other countries' hallmarks indicate origin, patent, manufacture, etc. Most of the countries in Europe stamped their gold and silver wares with "hallmarks". As early as 1363, England had already passed laws saying that every master goldsmith shall have a "quote by himself", and the same mark "shall be known by them which shall be assigned the King to survey their work allay". This meant that all the goldsmiths' work had to be assayed before they could put on the mark which was ordained by the King. Such marks would certify the ore content of both silver and gold.

By 1857, the word "sterling" became universally used except in the United States. Until 1894, no State protection was given to purchases of either gold or silver, and the buyer could only trust the reputation of the maker and dealer. [For a fuller explanation of HALLMARKS, see *100 Years of Collectible Jewelry, 1850-1950* by Lillian Baker]

Trademarks should not be confused with hallmarks. Trademarks identify a manufacturer or artisan; hallmarks guarantee the quality of the ore contained in the article, as well as the city and country vouching for same.
MARKS MISTAKEN FOR MANUFACTURER/DESIGNER/JEWELER:
[Rolled gold, silver plate or electro plate]
R.P.  = rolled plate
G.F.  = gold filled
G.S.  = German silver
E.P.  = silver electro plate
N.S.  = nickle silver
B.M.  = Britannia metal

## ILLUSION SETTING
A setting in which the stone is made to appear larger by cutting and shaping the metal mounting that surrounds the stone exactly like the base of the gem.

## JAPANNED
A process by which mourning pins made of iron wire were finished by immersing in black japan, a by-product of coal.

## "JARGOW-NIB"
A nickname used in 1913 for point-protectors. It was a comic "jab" at Berlin Police President von Jargold, who sought to enforce the wearing of hatpin "safeties" or "nibs", which would guard the dangerous points. Germany had stringent laws regarding the "hatpin danger".

## JET (genuine)
A brownish-black lignite in which the texture or grain of the original fossilized wood -- of which this particular coal is comprised -- can still be seen.

## JET (glass)
Often called "Black Glass Jewelry", it is an imitation of genuine Jet. This glass can be highly polished and intricately cut and faceted. Sometimes also known as "French Jet" or Bohemian "Black Glass Jewelry", in its perfected form it can be well classed not as an imitation of Jet -- which was its original intent -- but as an art glass highly regarded for its craftsmanship.

## MOSAIC

The art of creating a motif or design with small bits of colored glass or stone which are inlaid into mortar.

## NODDER

(Same as "bobbler", "springer", "trembler" or "tremblant") A short spring which causes the ornamental hatpin head to bounce freely atop the pin-shank.

## PASTE

A superior glass containing oxide of lead used for hatpin heads as imitation gems and gemstones. (Also called Strass, for its inventor, Josef Strasser).

## PAVE' SETTING

A setting in which the stones are placed so close together that almost no metal shows between them.

## PIERCEWORK

Die-cast frames which are cut and engraved with an interlacing of metal, in which there is a great deal of open-work.

## PIQUE

Inlaying of gold, silver, and mother-of-pearl overlay, or inlay of tortoise-shell, ivory, or horn.

## PLASTICS

Term applied to a group of synthetic chemical products with the distinctive quality which enables them to be molded, carved, laminated, or pressed into many shapes, sizes, and designs. Tortoise, horn, mother-of-pearl, wood, marble, jet, and amber were all imitated in plastics. Some imitations for natural elements were called by other names, such as in the imitation plastic "tortone" (tortoise), which was advertised as "non-breakable" by E. & J. Bass, New York; and "Tortoisene", manufactured by Harry Maynard, Washington, D.C.; Wm. K. Potter established his genuine Tortoise Shell Works at Providence, R.I., and horn and Celluloid were produced by Alfred Burke & Co., Leominster, Mass., and Thomas Long Co. of Boston. Besides "French Ivory" being produced, there was also "Ivoire Parisienne", both products being imitation ivory. As with fine French paste, plastic jewelry -- particularly of the Art Deco period -- was not really an imitation, but a legitmate art form.

## REPOUSSE' (See CHASING)

## RHINESTONE

At one time "rhinestones" meant rock crystals taken from the bed of the River Rhine, but this no longer applies. Thus, "rhinestone" takes it name but no element from the River Rhine, Germany. It is a faceted glass stone, usually set with foil or painted backing to give it highlights. It is inferior to French paste or strass, and once the foil backing is scratched or marred, it loses its luster.

**SETTING**
(See specific types: BEZEL, BOX, CHANNEL, CLAW, CROWN, GYPSY, ILLUSION and PAVE'.

**SILVER-DEPOSIT-WARE**
Glass decorated with silver overlay. Most popular in 1890, it was first made in 1880 by American manufacturer, Alvin Manufacturing Co., then copied for use in hatpin heads by originator and other companies. Alvin specialized in hatpins in 1893.

**STERLING (Also see HALLMARK)**
A British term referring to the highest standard of silver which has a fixed value of purity: 925 parts of silver with 75 parts of copper.

**STRASS (Also see PASTE and RHINESTONE)**
A brilliant lead glass used in creating artificial gems and gemstones. Named for Josef Strass (or Strasser), by whom it was perfected.

**TORTOISE-SHELL (Also see PLASTICS and PIQUE)**
Yellowish-brown grained substance which is the hardplate shell from the back of the tortoise. Imitation tortoise shell was manufactured from plastic. Sadler Bros., South Attleboro, Mass., made imitation "Tortoisene". Tortoise was used primarily for combs and hair ornaments, as well as some of the finest examples of nouveau jewelry. Commercial use of tortoise-shell referred to the products as "genuine tortoise", although the only portion utilized in manufacture of products for women's "vanity", was the carapice (or shell of the tortoise). Other portions of large sea-turtles were considered by some as edible delicacies.

**VANITY HEADS**
Hatpin heads which contain items associated with a woman's "vanity" or "conceit", i.e., mirror, perfume holder, powder pot with puff, rouge rag, etc.; the heads of hatpins opened and even contained small straight pins, or a watch, pillbox, coin holder, or compact. The year of the VANITY HATPIN was 1913, when they were widely advertised; these hatpins also had 10″ to 12″ pin-shanks, with additional length added by the ornamental head. VANITY HEADS were long in length and heavy in weight. Highly prized by collectors of hatpins as well as collectors of memorabilia.

- - - - -

# CHAPTER II

## HATPIN NOMENCLATURE

**Natural Elements as Ornamental Heads**
Abalone
Amber
Bog Oak
Bone
Claws (Falcon)
Copper
Coral
Feathers
Fur
Gems & Gemstones
Gold
Hair
Horn
Insect, (gilded or preserved)
Ivory
Jade
Jet
Mother-of-Pearl
Ores (alloys)
Pearls
Pods
Feet (Rabbit's)
Raffia
Rock Crystal (colorless quartz)
Roses (preserved and gilded)
Seeds
Shells
Silk
Silver
Skin (reptile)
Stone (not gem)
Straw
Tin
Tooth
Tortoise-Shell
Tusk
Wood (varieties, including petrified)
**Man-made and/or Manufactured Types of Hatpin Heads**
Advertising
Aesthetic Period (designs)
Amulet
Animal forms and figurals
Art Deco designs
Art Nouveau designs

Arts & Crafts Movement (designs)
Bead (single)
Beads
Beaded (cloth)
Billiken
Bird & Fowl forms and figurals
Blackamoor
Bobbler (Springer)
Bug (Insect) forms and figurals
Button (Glass and Metallic)
Cameo
Carnival Glass
Celtic designs
Celluloid
Charms
Charles Horner
Ceramic
Ceramic Transfer
China
Cloisonne
Coins
Commemorative
Crochet
Damascene
Decorated Glass
Emblems
Enamels
Escutcheon
Figural (See GLOSSARY)
Figural Mountings
Floral (Porcelain and Metallic)
French Ivory
Full Figural (See GLOSSARY)
Gift-boxed Sets
GLASS (blown, cut, etched, faceted, molded, pressed)
Specific Types
Art Nouveau and Art Deco designs
Glass bead with overlay
Glass beads, assorted
Glass, shoe-button type, black, white, blue
Glass, black (mourning)
Glass, burel (Czech.)
Glass, camphor
Glass, Carnival
Glass, clambroth
Glass, cobalt
Glass, colored
Glass, crystal
Glass, decorated

Glass, Dragon's Breath
Glass, enamelled
Glass, etched/engraved
Glass, figurals
Glass, free-form
Glass, goldstone
Glass, imitation gems & gemstones
Glass, iridescent
Glass, jet
Glass, jet riveted
Glass, lustre
Glass, mercury
Glass, milkglass (blue)
Glass, milkglass (decorated)
Glass, milkglass ("thorn" shape)
Glass, milkglass (white)
Glass, millefiori
Glass, mosaic
Glass, opaline
Glass, painted
Glass, French Pate de Vere
Glass, Peacock-Eye (foil)
Glass, pearl
Glass, pearlized lustre
Glass, Peking ("Poor Man's Jade" or "Canton Glass")
Glass, slag
Glass, thistle-cut
Glass, rhinestones
Glass, Venetian
Glass, wax-bead pearls
Leather
Metal alloys (tin, pewter, copper, chrome)
Plastics
Porcelain
Religious Symbols
Rhinestone (as overall design or accents)
Roses (gilded)
Satsuma-ware
Silver (Hallmarked)
Silver-Deposit-Ware
Souvenir
"Springer" (Same as "nodder", "tremblant", "bobbler", etc.)
Wax-bead Pearls
Wooden (carved, cut, lacquered, polished)
Woven straw
**Mountings for Hatpins**
Art Deco designs
Art Nouveau designs
Baroque designs

Cage-type
Chased
Claw-type
Crown-type
Filigree
Frame (See GLOSSARY)
Glass (rare)
Metallic (specifically for stones)
Patch or socket type
Pierced or open-work
Riveted on wire frame
Sleeve (bezel-set)
Socket (tubular or funnel type)
Span or bridge or arc type
Victorian designs
Wire-mounted
With escutheon plates on top
**Settings for Hatpin Stones**
bezel (or gypsy)
box
channel
claw
crown
illusion
metal cup
pave'
**Types of Pin-Shanks for Period Hatpins (4″ to 12″)**
Brass or gold color (gilt)
Clasp and hinged (safety-pin design)
Carat (or Karat) gold
Detachable (patented)
Hinged (patented)
Hiskins & Others company (double-prong, patented)
Japanned (black, for mourning)
Nickel (silver color)
Spiral (patented)
Steel (silver color)
Sterling (hallmarked), or marked "silver"
Tempered steel (greyish-blue)
Threaded (detachable)
"White" pin (steel, nickle, or alloy)
NODDERS with small spring attached. (Also called: "Bobbler",
"Springer", "Trembler", "Tremblant")
NIBS (guards, point-protector, or Jargow-nibs)
Brass with cork center to receive point
Ornamental with safety-spring. (Patented)
Brass Plunger-type, undecorated
Satsuma-ware, for use as ornament or nib
Plain brass with rubber insert to receive point

# SECTION IV.

## CHAPTER I
## EVALUATION

## CHAPTER II
## VALUE GUIDE

# CHAPTER I
## EVALUATING HATPINS AND HATPIN HOLDERS

*The current values in this handbook should be used only as a guide. They are not intended to set prices, which vary from one section of the country to another, and from one nation to another. Auction prices as well as dealer prices vary greatly, and are affected by the condition of the piece(s) as well as the demand for a particular period hatpin, china hatpin holder, or metallic hatpin stand. The values given in this handbook are for the exact item shown on a specific Plate, and the value is attributed to that particular collection. Neither the author nor the publisher assumes any responsibility for any losses that might be incurred as a result of consulting the value guide.*

A. HATPINS

The objective of a good price guide is to provide guidelines for retail pricing to collectors, dealers, appraisers, and others whose interest may rise out of mere curiosity.

Many considerations enter into placing a value on specific hatpins. Here are some of the more important ones.

The most collectible period hatpins are those with the longest pin-shanks, for they are usually hardest to find and most in demand by collectors. The period in which the longest pins were worn was also the shortest period of manufacture and demand of the fashions of the time. Because of laws regulating the size of pins, manufacturers produced fewer 12″ hatpins, and ladies -- not preferring to risk offending the law -- also purchased shorter and less hazardous designs, or else had the long hatpins cut down in length and re-sharpened.

Too, most of the longest hatpins were worn on extravagant hats which few could afford. Many hats ranged in price from $250.00, upward to several hundred, and only the very wealthy could discard hatpins when fashion so dictated. When this became the case, valuable gems which formerly graced a hatpin, were removed and set into other pieces of jewelry.

Celluloid hatpins are scarce because most collectors and dealers considered them hardly worthy of notice until the renewed interest in Art Deco of the roaring twenties, began to bring amazing prices.

Art Nouveau in any media is bringing higher prices than ever before, and this is true for hatpins and hatpin holders.

The "endangered species", such as walrus, elephant, whale, and tortoise, have made hatpins of tusk and shell soar in price.

The renewed interest in collectibles as a whole, enjoyed by more persons than ever before, has brought many new collectors into competition with longtime collectors of hatpins and hatpin holders. The founding of an international club for collectors of these objects, has spread the word as well.

These reasons have also provided impetus to some who "improvise" and supply imitations, newly contrived articles, fakes and reproductions of hatpins and hatpin holders.

Further enhancing hatpins and elevating their values, are the following;
ACCENTS
Beads as accents
Bell or rattle
Brilliants as accents
Eyes set with stones, glass or genuine
Gold or silver overlay
Handpainted accents, beading, or enamelling
Natural elements added as accents
Pearls of all kinds and sizes, added as accents
Small gems and gemstones
**Other Types of Accents or Additional Values**
Antiqued or oxidized metal
Art Deco design
Art Nouveau design
Artist's name (die-stamped)
Artist's signature (script)
Cloisonne or plique-a-jour
Manufacturer, distributor, and/or patent pending
A dated hatpin
Engraved initial, inscription or monogram
Hallmarks and/or initials
Glass imitation of gems and gemstones
Peacock eye glass
Handpainted china
Figural hatpins, such as Kewpie or Billikin
Advertising souvenirs
Vanity-top hatpins, such as for pins, compact, etc.
Gold or silver inlay, as in damascene or pique'
An inscription
Iridescent or art glass
Metallic accents
Natural elements such as 4-leaf clover or rabbit's foot
Religious symbols
Hatpins in pairs or boxed
Nodders or tremblants
Patented pin-shanks
Gift-boxed hatpins with matching studs, brooch, buckle, or veil pins
Charles Horner designs
Portraits in porcelain
Art Nouveau stylized women's heads
10″ to 12″ pin-shanks
Combination brooch and hatpin

## B. HATPIN HOLDERS

Porcelain or glass hatpin holders and metallic stands served the storage needs for hatpins. These were manufactured singly or as an added accessory to dresser sets, vanity sets, toilette sets, or commode combinations.

Beaded pincushions were also favored pieces used to skewer hatpins safely away, and they provided the perfect display for a bouquet of hatpins.

Except for reproductions and newly created molds produced as hatpin holders, the author has not found any type of hatpin receptacle under $22.50 in the seventies, and in this decade not a single porcelain hatpin holder for less than $32.50.

Prices for cut glass, Carnival, art glass, and jasper-ware, have soared along with prices of hallmarked sterling silver hatpin stands and the Royal Bayreuth, R.S. Prussia, S & V Mark, and figural hatpin holders.

Prices of hatpin holders have skyrocketed enough so that some collectors are forced to choose between collecting hatpins or hatpin holders. Or, they choose between majoring in one or the other.

Many old catalogues show hatpin holders being produced as late as the twenties, even after the cloche' was introduced which required no hatpins whatsoever. Instead, the hat styles of the twenties called for hat ornaments, and the hatpin holder was altered in appearance to accomodate hat ornaments with their various "nibs" which either screwed or plugged into the pointed end of the pin. The alteration to the hatpin holder consisted of doing away with the tiny pin-holes on top of the porcelain holder, and substituting either diagonal larger holes or even the open-top variety which were produced mainly in Japan. Some markings on the open-top holders show they were also made in the Bavarian area, and indicate they were of the Art Deco period when plastics and "French Ivory" were also becoming a favored material.

Rose Tapestry (Royal Bayreuth), Kewpie (German jasperware), S&V mark of Schaffer & Vater (Volkstedt-Rudolstadt area), Staffordshire area production (England), Carnival Glass (American), and R.S. Prussia (Red Mark), are probably the most collectible, desirable, and higher priced of the china or porcelain hatpin holders.

However, Nippon, (prior to "Made in Japan" markings), has probably taken one of the highest jumps in value. This is true of most Nippon-wares, but especially so in evaluating hatpin holders with handpainted scenes and those highly embellished with gold and fine moriage work.

Figural hatpin holders in any media, have always brought highest prices. Hatpins stands, as shown on the cover and pictured herein, are a delightful find and a more rare one, thus bringing high prices. This is especially true of hallmarked pieces.

Finely restored cushions on hatpin stands, do not devaluate the price on hatpin stands, nor do prices go down if beaded pincushions are similarly mended and/or restored. In fact, worn fabric and "bleeding straw" can detract asthetically and monetarily from any piece.

A mended or chipped porcelain or bisque hatpin holder definitely will bring a lower price; however, if the piece is unique and the piece is not too faulted, collectors will still want it enough to pay a fair price providing a deduction has been given because it is not mint.

Another factor which causes a rise in pricing, is the competition of other collectors, i.e., collectors of Carnival Glass v. collectors of hatpin holders only; collectors of Limoge, R.S. Prussia, Royal Bayreuth, and other marks v. collectors of marked hatpin holders only.

An artist's signature on handpainted porcelain, in addition to the manufacturer's mark, will add to the value of hatpin holders. This applies as well to a signature appearing on a metallic hatpin stand.

- - - -

For the past 18 months, and surely since the beginning of our new decade (1990's), an unexpected and astounding change has encroached upon the auction, shop, show, and general marketplace, reflecting sales and pricing of hatpins and hatpin holders.

Besides the spiraling changes in the pricing and sales of *period* hatpins and hatpin holders, demands of the new genre of hatpins and hat ornaments have created a completely new market and interest in hats and head-coverings. At least four fine makers of the "new vogue" hatpins have displayed expositions of lovely hatpins and hat ornaments. All of these artful renditions have been made "the old fashioned way," but with *new* findings, *new* pin-stems, and with no pretense at vending the pieces as either "old" or as "reproductions." Malls, bazaars, and boutiques of fine repute carry the designers' work and sell to an appreciative group of buyers who are cautioned to look for the unique, copyrighted signatures on each hatpin and/or hat ornament.

But then we find imposters who have flooded the marketplace in every major city and town where antique shows travel, with contrived marriages of pin-stems and buttons, buckles, and odds 'n ends of old jewelry. At first, when these fakes appeared in shops and shows, it was easy enough for an experienced collector to recognize these fakes and repros. Anyone who has read the author's books on the subject of hatpins and hatpin holders, will have learned how to recognize the frauds.

Unfortunately, in more recent cases it's been difficult to unmask the hatpin masquerading as a "period piece" because some manufacturers have begun to reproduce the old-time "findings" and have improved the workmanship and craftsmanship. One must now take close scrutiny of pieces, especially if in doubt. The lesson of buying from reputable dealers should be learned, now more than ever.

Auction prices, competition for the "period" pieces, and the growth of membership in the Int'l Club for Collectors of Hatpins and Hatpin Holders (founded by the author in 1977), have contributed to a high boom in prices. Demand influences "values" which translates into dollar-pricing. Another influence on pricing is the fact that overseas supplies are serving *domestic* needs instead of *export*.

As amazed as the author has become at the willingness of collectors to pay such higher prices, I must face stunning reality and adjust prices in the *Value Guide* to reflect the *real* market no matter how the market may leave one dumbfounded. It would be unfair to provide pricing for hatpins and holders that does *not* present a true picture even if it does not meet with what one may consider *fair*. After all, what people are willing to pay cannot be called unfair.

The author has, therefore, hit a happy medium by providing highs and lows, with the estimated true value somewhere in between. The prices herein *do not* attempt to reflect the *auction* place. Within the last 3 months, a hatpin was purchased at auction by a baseball enthusiast for almost $1,500! And figural Royal Bayreuth hatpins holders sold at auction to *Bayreuth collectors* from $1,000 tops to a "low" of $850!

As mentioned previousuly within the explanation of this Value Guide, collectors must compete with collectors of glass, and of Kewpies, and of just about every type and period piece. For what truly intrigues collectors of hatpins and hatpin holders, is that *this* collectible encompasses every imaginable natural and manmade element. That's what's so fascinating about the neverending, full-of-surprises collectibles called Hatpins and Hatpin Holders.

*Lillian Baker*

# Chapter II
# Value Guide

**Plate 1**
Row, 1, left to right.
Hatpin . . . . . . . . . . . $150.00-185.00
Hatpin . . . . . . . . . . . $145.00-165.00
Row 2, left to right.
Hatpin . . . . . . . . . . . $125.00-145.00
Hatpin . . . . . . . . . . . $155.00-195.00
Hatpin . . . . . . . . . . . $125.00-145.00
Row 3, left to right.
Hatpin . . . . . . . . . . . $125.00-155.00
Hatpin . . . . . . . . . . . $145.00-165.00
Hatpin . . . . . . . . . . . $125.00-155.00

**Plate 2**
Row 1, left to right.
Hatpin . . . . . . . . . . . $145.00-165.00
Hatpin . . . . . . . . . . . $75.00-85.00
Hatpin . . . . . . . . . . . $75.00-85.00
Row 2, left to right.
Hatpin . . . . . . . . . . . $55.00-65.00
Hatpin . . . . . . . . . . . $55.00-75.00
Hatpin . . . . . . . . . . . $65.00-85.00
Hatpin . . . . . . . . . . . $45.00-65.00
Row 3, left to right.
Hatpin . . . . . . . . . . . $110.00-135.00
Hatpin . . . . . . . . . . . $95.00-125.00
Hatpin . . . . . . . . . . . $65.00-85.00
Hatpin . . . . . . . . . . . $65.00-85.00
Hatpin . . . . . . . . . . . $110.00-135.00

**Plate 3**
Row 1, left to right.
Hatpin . . . . . . . . . . . $75.00-85.00
Hatpin . . . . . . . . . . . $55.00-75.00
Hatpin . . . . . . . . . . . $125.00-145.00
Hatpin . . . . . . . . . . . $55.00-65.00
Hatpin . . . . . . . . . . . $55.00-65.00
Row 2, left to right.
Hatpin . . . . . . . . . . . $45.00-65.00
Hatpin . . . . . . . . . . . $85.00-110.00
Hatpin . . . . . . . . . . . $45.00-65.00
Row 3, left to right.
Hatpin . . . . . . . . . . . $45.00-65.00
Hatpin . . . . . . . . . . . $45.00-55.00
Hatpin . . . . . . . . . . . $65.00-85.00
Hatpin . . . . . . . . . . . $65.00-85.00

**Plate 4**
Row 1, left to right.
Hatpin . . . . . . . . . . . $85.00-125.00
Hatpin . . . . . . . . . . . $75.00-110.00
Hatpin . . . . . . . . . . . $65.00-85.00

Row 2, left to right.
Hatpin . . . . . . . . . . . $135.00-150.00
Hatpin . . . . . . . . . . . $65.00-85.00
Row 3, left to right.
Hatpin . . . . . . . . . . . $65.00-85.00
Hatpin . . . . . . . . . . . $85.00-110.00
Hatpin . . . . . . . . . . . $45.00-55.00

**Plate 5**
Row 1, left to right.
Hatpin . . . . . . . . . . . $65.00-95.00
Hatpin . . . . . . . . . . . $65.00-95.00
Hatpin . . . . . . . . . . . $65.00-95.00
Row 2, left to right.
Hatpin . . . . . . . . . . . $75.00-110.00
Hatpin . . . . . . . . . . . $75.00-110.00
Row 3, left to right
Hatpin . . . . . . . . . . . $75.00-85.00
Hatpin . . . . . . . . . . . $95.00-125.00
Hatpin . . . . . . . . . . . $45.00-65.00

**Plate 6**
Row 1, left to right.
Hatpin Stand . . . . . . $150.00-175.00
Hatpin Stand . . . . . . $150.00-225.00
Row 2, left to right.
Hatpin Stand . . . . . . $175.00-250.00
Hatpin Stand . . . . . . $125.00-150.00
Row 3
Hatpin Stand . . . . . . $175.00-225.00
without hatpins.

**Plate 7**
Row 1, left to right.
Hatpin . . . . . . . . . . . $55.00-75.00
Hatpin . . . . . . . . . . . $85.00-110.00
Hatpin . . . . . . . . . . . $65.00-85.00
Row 2, left to right.
Hatpin . . . . . . . . . . . $55.00-75.00
Hatpin . . . . . . . . . . . $65.00-85.00
Hatpin . . . . . . . . . . . $85.00-125.00
Row 3, left to right.
Hatpin . . . . . . . . . . . $75.00-95.00
Hatpin . . . . . . . . . . . $75.00-85.00
Hatpin . . . . . . . . . . . $55.00-65.00
Row 4, left to right.
Hatpin . . . . . . . . . . . $65.00-85.00
Hatpin . . . . . . . . . . . $45.00-65.00
Hatpin . . . . . . . . . . . $65.00-85.00

**Plate 8**
Top
Hatpin . . . . . . . . . . . $65.00-85.00

Row 2, left to right.
Hatpin . . . . . . . . . . . . .$45.00-65.00
Hatpin . . . . . . . . . . . . .$45.00-65.00
Center
Hatpin . . . . . . . . . . . .$75.00-110.00
Bottom
Hatpin . . . . . . . . . . . . .$75.00-85.00

**Plate 9**
Top
Hatpin . . . . . . . . . . .$110.00-150.00
Row 2, left to right.
Hatpin . . . . . . . . . . . . .$55.00-65.00
Hatpin . . . . . . . . . . . . .$55.00-65.00
Center
Hatpin . . . . . . . . . . . .$85.00-125.00
Row 3, left to right
Hatpin . . . . . . . . . . . . .$65.00-85.00
Hatpin . . . . . . . . . . . . .$65.00-85.00
Row 4, left to right.
Hatpin . . . . . . . . . . . . .$65.00-85.00
Hatpin . . . . . . . . . . . . .$75.00-95.00
Hatpin . . . . . . . . . . . . .$75.00-95.00

**Plate 10**
Row 1, left to right.
Hatpin . . . . . . . . . . . . .$45.00-65.00
Hatpin . . . . . . . . . . . . .$45.00-55.00
Hatpin . . . . . . . . . . . . .$75.00-95.00
Hatpin . . . . . . . . . . . . .$30.00-40.00
Hatpin . . . . . . . . . . . . .$35.00-45.00
Hatpin . . . . . . . . . . . . .$35.00-45.00
Row 2, left to right.
Hatpin . . . . . . . . . . . . .$65.00-85.00
Hatpin . . . . . . . . . . . . .$40.00-55.00
Hatpin . . . . . . . . . . . . .$85.00-95.00
Row 3, left to right.
Stickpin . . . . . . . . . . .$55.00-75.00
Hatpin . . . . . . . . . . . .$95.00-110.00
Hatpin . . . . . . . . . . . . .$75.00-95.00
Hatpin . . . . . . . . . . . . .$75.00-95.00
Hatpin . . . . . . . . . . . . .$65.00-85.00
Row 4, left to right.
Hatpin . . . . . . . . . . . .$95.00-110.00
Hatpin . . . . . . . . . . . . .$65.00-85.00
Pin Stem . . . . . . . . . . .$45.00-55.00
Brooch . . . . . . . . . . . .$75.00-95.00

**Plate 11**
Row 1, left to right.
*Hatpin . . . . . . . . . . .$110.00-145.00
*Hatpin . . . . . . . . . . .$110.00-145.00
*Hatpin . . . . . . . . . . .$110.00-145.00
*Hatpin . . . . . . . . . . .$110.00-145.00

Hatpin . . . . . . . . . . . . .$75.00-85.00
(*Higher values because ivory from walrus
and elephant no longer available, as these
animals are on list of endangered species.)
Row 2, left to right.
Five Satsuma ware hatpins represent
widest ranges of prices: $145.00-250.00
average price each hatpin. Rarer ex-
amples, such as "Thousand Cranes" de-
signs, are $275.00-350.00. Satsuma ware
NIBS, $65.00-85.00; larger than ½" size,
$175.00-195.00. Rare.
Center
*Tortoise (piqué) . . . . . . .$85.00-125.00
Bottom, left to right.
*Tortoise . . . . . . . . . . .$75.00-95.00
*Tortoise . . . . . . . . . .$95.00-135.00
*Tortoise . . . . . . . . . .$185.00-225.00
*Tortoise . . . . . . .pr. $175.00-225.00
(*Endangered specie, and piqué work,
bring higher values.)

**Plate 12**
Left (Hatpin Holder w/3 hatpins)
Hatpin Holder . . . . . . .$85.00-125.00
Hatpins (2) . . . . . . .ea. $35.00-45.00
Hatpin (w/Brass Scarab) . $175.00-250.00
Top, left to right.
Hatpin . . . . . . . . . . . . .$35.00-65.00
Hatpin . . . . . . . . . . . . .$35.00-65.00
Hatpin . . . . . . . . . . . . .$45.00-75.00
Bottom, left to right.
Hatpin . . . . . . . . . . . . .$35.00-45.00
Hatpin . . . . . . . . . . . . .$55.00-85.00
Hatpin . . . . . . . . . . . . .$25.00-35.00
Hatpin . . . . . . . . . . . . .$25.00-45.00

**Plate 13**
Top, left to right.
Hatpin Holder . . . . . .$185.00-250.00
Hatpin Holder . . . . . .$150.00-225.00
Hatpin Holder . . . . . .$185.00-245.00
Row 2, left to right.
Hatpin Holder . . . . . . .$85.00-110.00
Hatpin Holder . . . . . .$165.00-210.00
Row 3, left to right.
Hatpin Holder . . . . . . .$65.00-85.00
Hatpin Holder . . . . . . .$65.00-85.00
Hatpin Holder . . . . . . .$85.00-95.00
Row 4, left to right.
Hatpin Holder . . . . . .$95.00-150.00
Hatpin Holder . . . . . .$75.00-125.00
Hatpin Holder . . . . . .$85.00-110.00
Hatpin Holder . . . . . . .$75.00-95.00

154

**Plate 14**
Vanity or Toilette Set, consisting of 8 pcs., (including cover to powder box ..............$495.00-550.00

**Plate 15**
Top
Vanity Set, 7 pcs., including lids to powder box and trinket box. . .$375.00-450.00
Bottom, right.
Hatpin Holder w/attached and covered trinket box ........$285.00-325.00

**Plate 16**
Top
Hatpin .............$95.00-150.00
Row 2, left to right.
Hatpin .............$85.00-110.00
Hatpin .............$85.00-110.00
Hatpin .............$85.00-110.00
Row 3, left to right.
Hatpin ...........$350.00-550.00
Hatpin ...........$95.00-125.00
Hatpin ...........$250.00-325.00
Bottom
Hatpin .............$85.00-110.00

**Plate 17**
Hatpin ...........$750.00-950.00
Must say "Pat. Pend" on inside.

**Plate 18A**
Hatpin Holder ......$375.00-450.00

**Plate 18B**
Hatpin Holder ......$475.00-575.00

**Plate 19**
Hatpins (pr. Charles Horner design), left and right: $75.00-110.00 each.
Center
Hatpin ..............$75.00-85.00

**Plate 20A**
Hatpin Holder ......$375.00-425.00

**Plate 20B**
Hatpin Holder ......$450.00-525.00

**Plate 21**
Five variations of hatpins, values ranging from $155.00-275.00. Rare.

**Plate 22**
Two vanity hatpins, ranging in values from ............ $350.00-450.00.

**Plate 23**
Hatpin ...........$450.00-550.00

**Plate 24A & 24B**
Hatpin (Moor's Head),
rare ............$450.00-600.00.

**Plate 25**
Hatpin ............$125.00-145.00

**Plate 26**
Hatpin (3 views), rare .$95.00-125.00

**Plate 27**
Hatpin Holder ......$185.00-275.00

**Plate 28**
Hatpin Holder ......$175.00-225.00
Stickpin Holder .....$135.00-150.00

**Plate 29**
Hatpin Holder ......$385.00-550.00

**Plate 30**
Hatpin Holder ......$185.00-225.00

**Plate 31**
Assorted riveted jet hatpins, values ranging from $185.00-325.00. Rare.

**Plate 32**
Hatpin Holder ......$225.00-285.00

**Plate 33**
Hatpin Holder ......$185.00-200.00

**Plate 34**
Hatpin ...........$250.00-375.00

**Plate 35**
Hatpin Holder ......$185.00-250.00

**Plate 36A**
Hatpin Holder ......$325.00-450.00

**Plate 36B**
Hatpin Holder ......$375.00-495.00

**Plate 37A & 37B**
Hatpin ............$85.00-125.00

**Plate 38**
Hatpin Holder . . . . . .$285.00-325.00

**Plate 39**
Hatpin . . . . . . . . . . . . .$95.00-135.00

**Plate 40**
Hatpin . . . . . . . . . . . . . $75.00-95.00

**Plate 41**
Hatpin . . . . . . . . . . . . .$75.00-110.00

**Plate 42**
Hatpin . . . . . . . . . . . . .$95.00-135.00

**Plate 43**
Hatpin . . . . . . . . . . . . . $65.00-75.00

**Plate 44A**
Hatpin Holder . . . . . .$135.00-155.00

**Plate 44B**
Hatpin Holder . . . . . .$175.00-225.00

**Plate 44C**
Hatpin Holder . . . . . .$165.00-195.00

**Plate 44D**
Hatpin Holder . . . . . .$185.00-250.00

**Plate 45A**
Hatpin Holder . . . . . .$185.00-250.00

**Plate 45B**
Hatpin Holder . . . . . .$375.00-495.00

**Plate 45C**
Hatpin Holder . . . . . .$150.00-185.00

**Plate 45D**
Hatpin Holder . . . . . .$135.00-145.00

**Plate 46A**
Hatpin & Stickpin combination holder
. . . . . . . . . . . . . . . . .$145.00-185.00

**Plate 46B**
Hatpin Holder . . . . . .$125.00-145.00

**Plate 46C**
Hatpin Holder . . . . . .$125.00-145.00

**Plate 46D**
Hatpin Holder . . . . . .$145.00-175.00

**Cover**
Vanity of Dresser Set, consisting of 11 pcs., including covered trinket boxes and pr. of candlesticks (not shown). {Author's Collection} .$550.00-850.00

Hatpin Stand (center), containing a concealed jewelry compartment under plus velvet cushion. {Milly Combs Collection} . . . . . . . . . . . . . $250.00-285.00

Hatpin Stand, (tall), upper right, containing Charles Horner designed hatpins. Hatpin Stand accented with amythest color thistle – but stone. (Stand only) {Dena Archer Collection} . . .$250.00-285.00

Charles Horner hatpins in both hatpin stands {Author's Collection} range in values from . . . . . . . .$125.00-175.00

Safety-pin type hatpin w/peacock eye accent. {Milly Combs Collection}
. . . . . . . . . . . . . . . .$110.00-145.00

Assorted porcelain, iridescent, figural, mosaic, rhinestone, hand-painted hatpins from Archer, Combs and Author's Collections . . . . . . . . . . .$75.00-225.00

Art Nouveau Lady with Calla Lily, and Winged Cherub tumbling on head, from author's collection. {NFS}

# SECTION V

## CHAPTER I
## RECOMMENDED READING

## CHAPTER II
## REFERENCE NOTES, CREDITS,
## & ACKNOWLEDGEMENTS

## CHAPTER I

(Although some of the books listed below are out-of-print, they are usually available through reference libraries.)

## RECOMMENDED READING

ANSCOMBE, ISABELLEand CHARLOTTE GERE, *Arts and Crafts in Britain and America,* Rizzoli International Publications, Inc., New York. (1978)

BAKER, LILLIAN, *The Collector's Encyclopedia of Hatpins and Hatpin Holders,* Collector Books, Paducah, KY (1976)

BAKER, LILLIAN, *One Hundred Years of Collectible Jewelry, (1850-1950),* Collector Books, Paducah, KY (Revised 1983)

BAKER, LILLIAN, *Art Nouveau & Art Deco Jewelry,* Collector Books, Paducah, KY (1981)

BAUER, DR. JAROSLAV, *Minerals, Rocks and Precious Stones,* Octopus Books Limited, London. (1974)

BRADBURY, FREDERICK, F.S.A., *Bradbury's Book of Hallmarks,* J.W. Northend Ltd., West Street, Sheffield, S13SH, England. (1975)

FRANCIS, JR., PETER, *The World of Beads Monograph Series, 1 thru 5,* Lapis Route Books, Cornerless Cube, Box 630, Lake Placid, N.Y. 12946. (1979-1982)

HASLAM, MALCOLM, *Marks and Monograms of the Modern Movement, 1875-1930,* Charles Scribner's Sons. (1977)

HILLIER, BEVIS, *Art Deco of the 20s and 30s,* Studio Vista/Dutton, New York. (1968)

HUGHES, GRAHAM, *The Art of Jewelry,* The Viking Press, Inc., 625 Madison Ave., New York, NY 10022. (1972)

JULIAN, PHILIPE, *The Triumph of Art Nouveau Paris Exhibition 1900,* Larousse & Co., Inc. 572 Fifth Ave., New York, (1974)

NEWBLE, BRIAN, *Practical Enamelling and Jewelry Work,* The Viking Press, 625 Madison Ave., New York. (1967)

VAN PATTEN, JOAN F., *The Collector's Encyclopedia of Nippon Porcelain,* (Series 1 and 2). Collector Books, Paducah, KY (1979-1982)

WYNTER, HARRIET, *An Introduction to European Porcelain,* Thomas Y. Crowell Company, New York. (1971)

NOTE: COLLECTOR BOOKS, (A Division of Schroeder Publishing Co. Inc.), has a series of encyclopedias on porcelains relative to the subject of this handbook, and all are recommended reading. Send to COLLECTOR BOOKS for a complete listing and order blank.

## CHAPTER II
## REFERENCE NOTES

**Title**

*Vol. IV, 15th Edition, 1975 Encyclopaedia Brittanica,* Encyclopedia Publishing Co., Chicago, IL.

*"MS" Magazine,* (Sept. 1972), "MS" Magazine Corp., New York.

*"Aurora Leigh, Book VIII",* Elizabeth Barrett Browning, Crowell Publishing, 1900.

*"The Men of the Alamo",* (Poems of American History), published by Riverside Press, Cambridge, MA.

*"A Prologue to Love",* Taylor Caldwell, Bantam, 1973.

*"The Year of the Horse",* Eric Hatch, Crown Publishers, Inc., New York. 1965.

*"The Sin Mark",* Margaret Page Hood, Coward-McCann, Inc. New York.

*"Truly Emily Post",* Edwin Post, Funk & Wagnalls Co., 1961.

*"George",* Emlyn Williams, Random House, 1961.

*"Jennie",* Ralph G. Martin, Prentice-Hall, Inc., Englewood, NJ.

*"The Trembling Hills",* Phyllis A. Whitney, Ace Books, Inc. New York.

## CREDITS & ACKNOWLEDGMENTS

Unless otherwise noted, all drawings and illustrations are from the talented pen of Joyce Fairchild.

The author expresses her gratitude for the kindness, courtesy, interest and assistance of the following whose photographs of haptins and holders from their collections appear in this book:

Dena Archer, Shirley Babcock, Milly Combs, Doris Gaston, Barbara Hammell, Audrae Heath, Carol King, and Robert V. Larsen.

Many thanks to those who offered photographs for inclusion. The gesture is truly appreciated; however, because of specific publishing requirements, some could not be used.

Special acknowledgment is given to all the photographers and illustrators whose names are credited individually for their excellent work and contribution made to this publication. The author extends extra earned praise for the patience and cooperation of Dave and Barbara Lee Hammell, which made possible the excellence of the color Cover and Plates.

Kudos to Bill and Meredith Schroeder, my publishers, and to their superior staff at COLLECTOR BOOKS, for their efforts and continued confidence in my work

And to the scores of persons, organizations, and companies far and wide, whose correspondence and contacts aided in the publication of the author's encyclopedic work and this subsequent handbook, the author extends a second salutation--heartfelt thanks!

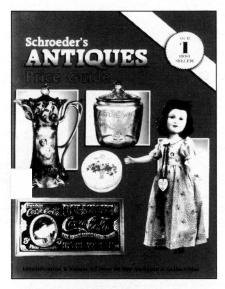